The media's watching Vault!
Here's a sampling of our coverage.

"For those hoping to climb the ladder of success, [Vault's] insights are priceless."
– *Money magazine*

"The best place on the Web to prepare for a job search."
– *Fortune*

"[Vault guides] make for excellent starting points for job hunters and should be purchased by academic libraries for their career sections [and] university career centers."
– *Library Journal*

"The granddaddy of worker sites."
– *U.S. News & World Report*

"A killer app."
– *The New York Times*

One of *Forbes'* 33 "Favorite Sites"
– *Forbes*

"To get the unvarnished scoop, check out Vault."
– *Smart Money Magazine*

"Vault has a wealth of information about major employers and job-searching strategies as well as comments from workers about their experiences at specific companies."
– *The Washington Post*

"A key reference for those who want to know what it takes to get hired by a law firm and what to expect once they get there."
– *New York Law Journal*

"Vault [provides] the skinny on working conditions at all kinds of companies from current and former employees."
– *USA Today*

VAULT
> the most trusted name in career information™

VAULT CAREER GUIDE TO
NURSING

VAULT CAREER GUIDE TO
NURSING

MELINDA JENKINS
AND THE STAFF OF VAULT

FREE PUBLIC LIBRARY, SUMMIT, N.J.

For information about permission to reproduce selections from this book, contact Vault Inc., 150 W. 22nd St., 5th Floor, New York, NY 10011, (212) 366-4212.

Library of Congress CIP Data is available.

ISBN 13: 978-1-58131-503-5

ISBN 10: 1-58131-503-1

Printed in the United States of America

ACKNOWLEDGMENTS

Vault's acknowledgments: We are extremely grateful to Vault's entire staff for all their help in the editorial, production and marketing processes. Vault also would like to acknowledge the support of our investors, clients, employees, family and friends. Thank you!

Table of Contents

Nursing Uppers and Downers   65

A Day in the Life of a Nurse   73

APPENDIX   87

Visit Vault at **www.vault.com** for insider company profiles, expert advice,
career message boards, expert resume reviews, the Vault Job Board and more.

VAULT CAREER LIBRARY   **xi**

Losing sleep over your job search?
Endlessly revising your resume?
Facing a work-related dilemma?

Introduction

Nurses do not wear those funny hats anymore!

Nursing is a broad and exciting science field with tremendous career rewards, such as good starting salaries and easy mobility to various specialties and locations. Nurses are problem solvers who enjoy working with people and serving society. The worldwide demand for nurses both in and out of hospitals is currently extremely strong and is expected to grow for the next 15 years or more; at the moment, there are over 2.4 million nurses in the U.S. Because of the great demand, nurses are able to easily change positions to adapt to life changes, and many nurses work in several specialties both inside and outside hospitals in the course of their careers.

THE SCOOP

The History of Nursing

The International Council of Nurses defines the nursing career as encompassing "autonomous and collaborative care of individuals of all ages, families, groups and communities, sick or well and in all settings. Nursing includes the promotion of health, prevention of illness, and the care of ill, disabled and dying people. Advocacy, promotion of a safe environment, research, participation in shaping health policy and in patient and health systems management, and education are also key nursing roles."

The Birth of the Nursing Industry

Nursing was in some way practiced in nearly every civilization as family and community groups worked to care for their ill and dependent members. Early Christians combined charity and the care of the sick and poor in some of the first hospitals in Europe where women provided nursing care. Nurses also worked in their communities outside the hospital in ways very similar to physicians. However, social and professional status for long periods of history was driven by gender, class and religion, limiting the acceptance of nursing, or any women's occupation, as a true profession. Predominantly working class women, nurses were greatly constrained by gender inequities in society. Cultural norms deemed the respected professions of theology, law and medicine as proper for men, not for women. In addition, women working with the bodies of men, even in a healing occupation, were looked down upon. Things began to change in the U.S. in the 1940s during World War II when nurses became the first women in military service. Also, during WW II, women in the U.S. and European countries gained employment in factories and other areas while many men were away at war. Since the women's movement in the 1960s, the profession of nursing has gained much in stature. After the 1960s, nursing education moved away from a hospital apprenticeship model to a university-based model, emphasizing the sciences and practice based on research.

The first modern nurses

Florence Nightingale, a British citizen, is considered to be the founder of modern nursing. She brought basic notions of sanitation, nutrition and documentation to care for the sick and wounded soldiers in the Crimean War in the 1860s. The Crimean War was fought near the Black Sea in what is now

Visit Vault at **www.vault.com** for insider company profiles, expert advice, career message boards, expert resume reviews, the Vault Job Board and more.

VAULT CAREER LIBRARY   5

the Ukraine and part of Turkey. France, the United Kingdom, the Ottoman Empire and Sardinia were allied against Russia. Later, she founded a school of nursing in England, which is now part of King's College of London, where women could take up a respectable profession. (For many years, acceptable occupations for women, mostly unmarried women, in the U.S. were limited to nursing, teaching, secretarial and shop keeping.) The history in related English-speaking countries is similar. New Zealand began Registration of Nursing in 1901, and Ellen Dougherty was the first name written in the book; she became the first registered nurse in the world. England began nursing registration in 1919.

Over the past century, several community nurses developed autonomous nursing centers that provide a model for today. Lillian Wald, Margaret Sanger and Mary Breckinridge were pioneers in providing direct access to what is now known as nurse-managed care. Direct access means that any person can select and pay a nurse directly, and does not have to go indirectly through a physician or hospital to have them order nursing care. Each of these pioneers sought to provide needed services to underserved populations during a similar time—what appears to be the heyday of public health before private health care became lucrative.

With her colleague Mary Brewster, Lillian Wald founded the Visiting Nurse Service (VNS), which exists today in New York City. Visiting nurses, then and now, visit people in their homes to provide care. Originally, they were hired and paid directly by the families. Today, most visiting nurses are paid by the federal Medicare program to care for people recently released from the hospital. Medicare rules, negotiated by the American Medical Association in the 1960s, require a physician's order for home care nursing. In 1895, Wald and Brewster opened the nurse-managed Henry Street Settlement, a community center for health and wellness still in operation under the auspices of Pace University School of Nursing. By 1915, 100 Settlement nurses had made over 227,000 visits to more than 26,000 patients. Wald pushed for the establishment of the U.S. Children's Bureau, which eventually evolved into the current Bureau of Maternal-Child Health. In addition, she created the national district nursing service of the Red Cross.

Margaret Sanger and her sister Ethel opened the first birth control clinic in the U.S. in Brooklyn in 1916. After nine days in operation, the clinic was closed and Sanger was arrested and imprisoned. As a result of her legal appeal, physicians were allowed to prescribe contraceptive information for medical reasons. So, in 1923 Sanger opened another birth control clinic run by a physician. In 1939, the American Birth Control League (founded by Sanger), merged with the Birth Control Clinical Research Bureau and became the present-day Planned Parenthood Federation of America. And in 1952, Sanger helped found the International Planned Parenthood Federation.

Mary Breckinridge and two nurse colleagues, Freida Caffin and Edna Rockstroh, established the Frontier Nursing Service (FNS) in 1925 in Leslie County, Kentucky. Nurse-midwives who had trained in England rode on horseback over hill and stream to provide prenatal care and to attend births at remote Appalachian homes. In 1939, Breckinridge opened the first nurse-midwifery school in the United States, the Frontier Graduate School of Midwifery. Today, graduate education for family nurse practitioners is also offered. Demonstrating national professional leadership, the American College of Nurse Midwives was founded by Frontier Nursing Service staff in 1929.

Today's nurse-managed centers, numbering about 200, are mostly in urban and inner-city areas. Most were initiatives funded by the U.S. Health Resources Administration, Division of Nursing, in order to provide learning laboratories for NP students. They are owned or affiliated with schools of nursing who oversee the hiring of staff (usually NPs and support staff) and overall management. Centers are primarily based at community sites, including nursing schools, elementary and secondary schools, colleges, senior or neighborhood centers, public housing neighborhoods, shelters, churches, storefronts, hospitals, mobile vans and other commercial locations. The centers provide primary health care, including screening and health maintenance, diagnosis and management of acute and chronic diseases, care coordination and referral, and group health education. The majority of patients are from culturally diverse and vulnerable populations, including persons over age 85, non-English speaking, homeless, victims of abuse, substance abusers, mentally ill, HIV-positive, migrants, developmentally disabled or handicapped.

Nursing practice has changed a great deal in the past century. Nurse anesthetists were the first advanced practice nurses from the late 1800s, followed by nurse midwives in the early 1920s, clinical nurse specialists in the 1950s and nurse practitioners (NPs) in the 1960s.

Nurse practitioners

NPs were formally created in 1965. In 1979, Alaska and Washington were the first states to legislate prescriptive authority for NPs, and now, NPs can prescribe medications in all 50 states. In 14 states, NPs can prescribe (including controlled substances) independently of any required physician

Visit Vault at **www.vault.com** for insider company profiles, expert advice, career message boards, expert resume reviews, the Vault Job Board and more.

V/\ULT CAREER LIBRARY　　7

involvement. In all states, NPs may receive and/or dispense drug samples. NPs in several other countries, including Ireland, New Zealand and England, also have prescriptive authority.

The History of Nursing Education

Based on the Nightingale model, training schools for nurses were set up in the U.S. and other countries. The training schools were run by hospitals and nursing students provided service to the hospital in an apprenticeship. In 1923, Yale School of Nursing evolved from the Connecticut Training School to become the first autonomous school of nursing in the U.S. Yale School of Nursing, still operating today, has its own dean, faculty, budget and degree according to university standards. In keeping with a national study of nursing education, the Goldmark Report, collegiate nursing education was promoted over apprenticeship training in a hospital. After this point, nursing education and student learning needs broke from hospital service.

Two-year associate degree education for RNs began in the 1950s, intended as a short-term fix for a post-war nursing shortage. Currently, all three types of degrees coexist with a new variant of second-degree, also known as "accelerated" baccalaureate, consisting of approximately two years of nursing study after a previous bachelor's degree. All of these types of education qualify an individual to take the national RN licensing exam, known as the NCLEX. However, only baccalaureate or post-baccalaureate education prepares one for career and educational advancement. Therefore, most professional nursing organizations support baccalaureate programs.

The first bachelor's degree in nursing was conferred at Yale University School of Nursing in 1937. Yale subsequently developed a master's degree to prepare nurses for leadership positions and careers in management and education. Columbia University was the first to award a doctoral degree in nursing education (the EdD, at Teachers College) in 1924, and the first to award a graduate degree in a clinical nursing specialty in 1956.

New York University was the first to award a degree in nursing research; it was the PhD, or Doctor of Philosophy. The first Doctor of Nursing Science (DNS or DNSc) degree, also a research degree, was awarded by Boston University. Today, the premier federal research institution, the National Institutes of Health (NIH), includes the National Institute of Nursing Research, founded in 1985, which has a budget of nearly $150 million to fund nursing research. Nurse researchers also obtain funding from other NIH centers and institutes, as well as from foundations, industry and other sources.

Doctor of Nursing Practice (DNP or DrNP) degrees are promoted by the American Association of Colleges of Nursing to prepare clinical or management experts skilled in directing and coordinating patient care. DNPs are becoming more prevalent since beginning in 1998 at the University of Tennessee-Memphis. A few years later, DNP programs began at the University of Kentucky and Rush University in Chicago. It is expected that eventually the DNP degree will replace the master's degree for NPs. About 15 programs are now enrolling students seeking the DNP; another 190 programs are under development.

Nursing Careers Today

Nursing careers have come a long way. Types of modern nurses include registered nurses (RNs), who are college educated, with one of the following: a four-year Bachelor of Science in Nursing (BSN); an "accelerated" one- to two-year second baccalaureate degree (BSN); or a two-year associate's degree in nursing (ADN). Sometimes BSNs are called "registered professional nurses" and ADNs are called "registered technical nurses." Today, nurses are increasingly prepared with collegiate bachelor's, master's and doctoral degrees. National statistics show that ADNs, though they make up about half of all nurses in the U.S., rarely advance their education and rarely hold positions above staff level. Therefore, a BSN is considered the best basic nursing preparation upon which to build a rewarding career.

Advanced degrees

Advanced practice nurses (APNs) include several types: nurse practitioners (NP), a BSN with a master's degree; certified nurse midwives (CNM), a BSN with a master's degree; certified nurse anesthetists (CRNA), a BSN with a master's degree; clinical nurse specialists (CNS), a BSN with a master's degree; clinical nurse leader (CNL), a BSN with a master's degree. In 2004, the number of RNs prepared to practice in at least one advanced practice role was estimated to be 240,461, or 8.3 percent of the total RN population. Fifty-one percent are NPs, 24 percent are CNSs, 13 percent are CRNAs, 4 percent are CNMs, and 8 percent are combinations of two or more specialties.

Registered Nurses Prepared for Advanced Practice, March 2004

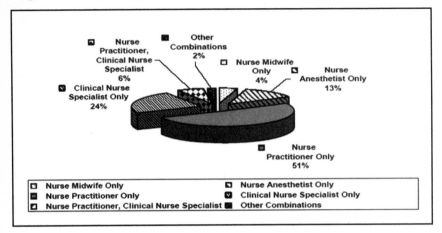

from: bhpr.hrsa.gov/healthworkforce/reports/nursing/samplesurvey04preliminary/default.htm

Doctors of Nursing Practice (DNP) are BSNs with a clinical doctorate, similar to a clinical psychologist or physical therapist. Doctorally-prepared nurse researchers/educators are BSNs with a doctoral degree such as a Doctor of Philosophy (PhD) or Doctor of Nursing Science (DNS or DNSc).

Other nursing support staff workers have many limitations in the job market, such as low pay, strenuous work and rotating shift schedules. They include: licensed practical nurses (LPN), with a one-year technical education, and nurse's aides, with varying education of usually a few weeks. Contrary to prevalent public perception, national statistics show that these support staff positions do not readily lead up the career ladder to the much better-paid registered nurse. Often, the collegiate educational requirements for a BSN are too strenuous to allow credit for courses previously taken for supporting staff roles.

Industry Trends

CHAPTER 2

Health care is one of the strongest sectors of the American economy. Indeed, some believe it is currently driving the economy. There is a great demand for nurses that is projected to continue for at least the next 15 years. Given the trend toward an aging population, there is an especial need for nurses to work in home care and long-term care, as well as hospitals. Nurses who speak a second language beyond English are extremely well suited to provide care in many parts of the U.S. As the industry moves toward focusing payment on evidence-based care, well-educated nurses who know how to access current information and are continuing their learning will be the most valuable and will earn top salaries.

According to the U.S. Department of Labor, the average annual salary for RNs was $52,330 in May 2004. Three out of five jobs for RNs are in hospitals. However, because less expensive alternatives to hospital care, such as home care and outpatient care, are growing, more new RN jobs are expected outside of hospitals. Generally, RNs with at least a bachelor's degree will have better job prospects than those without a bachelor's. In addition, all four advanced practice specialties—clinical nurse specialists, nurse practitioners, midwives and anesthetists—will be in high demand, particularly in medically underserved areas such as inner cities and rural areas. Relative to physicians, these RNs increasingly serve as lower-cost primary care providers.

Exciting New Developments in Health Care

The nursing industry is always evolving. Although the personal attention to patients and other fundamental qualities remains constant, developments in how we provide health care, such as direct reimbursement and retail pharmacy walk-in clinics, directly affect nursing careers.

Direct reimbursement

Direct reimbursement, payment directly to the nurse for care provided, was legislated for federal Medicaid and Medicare programs and many private insurers have followed suit. Direct reimbursement for nurse practitioners and nurse midwives through the federal/state Medicaid program for low-income Americans was legislated in 1989. Federal law mandates direct reimbursement to pediatric (PNP) and family (FNP) nurse practitioners providing services to children. NPs may be paid whether or not they collaborate with a physician; in other words, NPs may work independently. The NP care billed under Medicaid is considered equivalent to physician care. It is the responsibility of each state to determine its reimbursement rate for nurse practitioners and physicians. Even though the law mandates reimbursement to pediatric and family NPs, individual states may also opt to reimburse the services provided by other nurse practitioner specialties (i.e., geriatric, neonatal and adult NPs).

Direct reimbursement through Medicare was legislated in 1997 in the federal Balanced Budget Act. When a person with Medicare visits an NP or CNS instead of a physician, direct payment to the NP or CNS is 85 percent of the Medicare physician fee schedule amount. For example, Jane Smith FNP, has a private practice; when she sees a patient over age 65, she may bill Medicare and receive 85 percent of the Medicare physician fee for that equivalent service. Alternatively, if Jane Smith works "incident to" the primary physician caring for the Medicare patient, the physician will follow certain rules and be authorized to bill for the care.

NPs have received direct reimbursement from federal Medicaid and Medicare, as well as a number of private health insurers. CNMs, CNSs and CRNAs also receive direct reimbursement in many areas. When nurses receive payment directly, rather than through an employer or a physician, they have the ability to run their own businesses.

See the American Academy of Nurse Practitioners web site, legislation and practice section, for detailed information on laws and issues that pertain to direct reimbursement from all sources

Nurse-managed centers

The following are some of the businesses that NPs run with direct payment and with funding from schools of nursing and other agencies. Currently there are an estimated 200 nurse-managed centers, most affiliated with schools of nursing and providing primary health care as well as clinical training for nursing and other health occupations. Many nurse-managed centers have joined together to promote their work. The National Nursing Centers Consortium (NNCC) represents nurse-managed health centers serving vulnerable people across the country (nncc.us) and The Institute for Nursing Centers—INC—(www.nursingcenters.org) is developing a national data system for nursing centers. The founding members of the INC are the

Michigan Academic Consortium, the American Association of Colleges of Nursing, the Nursing Centers Research Network, the Michigan Primary Care Association, the National Nursing Center Consortium (NNCC), and the National Organization of Nurse Practitioner Faculties.

Retail pharmacy walk-in clinics

These have suddenly gained momentum and are springing up all over the country. They are not usually owned or managed by NPs but they do employ NPs to provide basic, fast care for common acute problems such as cough, fever and minor injuries. Their locations in retail pharmacies and groceries are meant to be convenient and they are low-cost for people without health insurance.

Alternative care

Many nurses combine their education in Western allopathic medical care with alternative care, such as nutritional therapy, yoga or massage. The market for alternative care is large and consumers are willing to pay out-of-pocket for these services when they are not covered by health insurance. Nurses are ideal providers of alternative care because of their solid education in physiology, nutrition, health risk assessment and cross-cultural aspects of care. They combine knowledge of Western medicine with alternatives and can judge the safety of combining the two. Even when nurses do not provide alternative therapy themselves, they often have helpful information about the modalities and practitioners of a variety of therapies. Research on NPs showed that 9 out of 10 referred patients when relevant to a variety of alternative providers for massage therapy, chiropractic care, acupuncture or acupressure, nutritional therapy and herbal treatment.

Visit Vault at **www.vault.com** for insider company profiles, expert advice, career message boards, expert resume reviews, the Vault Job Board and more.

VAULT CAREER LIBRARY   13

Shortage

The shortage of RNs nationwide is predicted to increase 41 percent from 2000 to 2020. Projected shortages vary by state, depending on current supply and population demographics. The largest shortages are predicted to be in settings that serve the elderly (such as home health care and nursing homes) and in hospital outpatient settings. Economists have pointed out that the wages of nurses, while seemingly fair, have not increased in real terms over the past 20 years.

Actual and "Real" Average Annual Salaries of Full-Time Registered Nurses

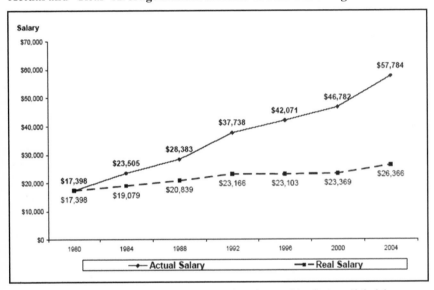

from: bhpr.hrsa.gov/healthworkforce/reports/nursing/samplesurvey04preliminary/default.htm

In 2004, the RN shortage was least in New England with 1,107 employed RNs per 100,000 population. The area with the next best supply of RNs was the West North Central (Iowa, Kansas, Minnesota, Missouri, Nebraska, North Dakota). The two areas with the lowest concentration were the West South Central (Arkansas, Louisiana, Oklahoma, Texas) and the Pacific area (Alaska, California, Hawaii, Oregon, Washington). The reasons for these differences are not well defined.

Baseline Projections of Demand for FTE RNs

Setting	2000	2005	2010	2015	2020	Increase from 2000-2020
Total [a]	2,001,500	2,161,300	2,347,100	2,569,800	2,824,900	41%
Hospitals [a]	1,239,500	1,324,800	1,427,900	1,555,600	1,698,900	37%
Short-term hospital, inpatient	874,700	930,200	999,100	1,086,800	1,187,000	36%
Short-term hospital, outpatient	83,500	95,900	110,400	126,400	142,000	70%
Short-term hospital, emergency	90,300	92,200	94,500	97,300	100,400	11%
Long-term hospitals	191,000	206,500	223,900	245,100	269,400	41%
Nursing facilities	172,800	197,200	224,500	253,600	287,300	66%
Physician offices	155,000	166,400	178,800	191,600	204,700	32%
Home health	132,000	157,300	187,500	226,200	275,600	109%
Occupational health	20,200	21,000	22,000	23,100	23,900	18%
School health	57,600	59,700	60,400	61,100	62,200	8%
Public health	99,800	103,500	107,300	111,500	115,800	16%
Nurse education	45,900	49,600	53,800	58,800	64,500	41%
Other health care	78,500	81,700	84,900	88,400	92,000	17%

[a] *Due to rounding, category totals might fail to equal the sum across component settings.*

Exhibit 24. Projected U.S. FTE RN Supply, Demand and Shortages

	2000	2005	2010	2015	2020
Supply	1,890,700	1,942,500	1,941,200	1,886,100	1,808,000
Demand	2,001,500	2,161,300	2,347,000	2,569,800	2,824,900
Shortage	(110,800)	(218,800)	(405,800)	(683,700)	(1,016,900)
Supply ÷ Demand	94%	90%	83%	73%	64%
Demand Shortfall	6%	10%	17%	27%	36%

(bhpr.hrsa.gov/healthworkforce/reports/behindrnprojections/behindshortage.htm)

Visit Vault at **www.vault.com** for insider company profiles, expert advice, career message boards, expert resume reviews, the Vault Job Board and more.

VAULT CAREER LIBRARY

15

Foreign-Educated Nurses

Foreign-educated nurses must obtain a work visa to work in the United States. The international Commission on Graduates of Foreign Nursing Schools (CGFNS International) will review their education, and they must pass a nursing certification and English proficiency exam (unless they are from an English-speaking country, including Australia, Canada [except Quebec], Ireland, New Zealand and the United Kingdom). In addition to the national review and examination, many states have related requirements.

Only 3.5 percent of RNs in the U.S. in 2004 were foreign-educated; half come from the Philippines and another 20 percent come from Canada. Other countries where RNs were educated include the United Kingdom, Nigeria, Ireland, India, Hong Kong, Jamaica, Israel and South Korea. About 12 percent of foreign-educated RNs working in the U.S. are from 47 other countries.

CGFNS International (www.cgfns.org) is the best resource for foreign-educated nurses who would like to work in the U.S. One can get information about qualifications, visa applications and RN licensure in each of the 50 states. The web site accepts online applications for the U.S. RN licensure examination. Over the past 30 years, CGFNS International has certified the credentials of over 400,000 foreign-educated nurses and other health care professionals for U.S. licensure and immigration.

Country of Origin for Foreign-Educated RNs in 2004

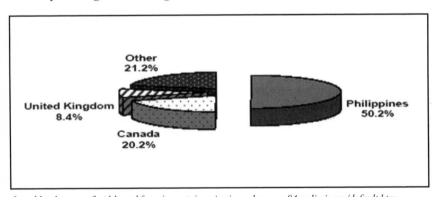

Other
21.2%

United Kingdom
8.4%

Canada
20.2%

Philippines
50.2%

from bhpr.hrsa.gov/healthworkforce/reports/nursing/samplesurvey04preliminary/default.htm

Nursing Specialties

Nurses work both inside and outside hospitals. Typical nursing jobs include medical-surgical nurses caring for hospitalized people, nurse practitioners providing outpatient care for chronic diseases and RNs supervising support staff in long-term care facilities. A variety of full-time, part-time and flexible-hours positions are available around the world for nurses educated in the United States. Demand and salaries for nurses are rapidly growing in the U.S. By 2020, the demand is expected to be nearly double that of 2005.

Clinical specialties in nursing correspond with many medical specialties, such as medical-surgical, pediatrics, women's health, geriatrics, family practice, intensive care, home care, long-term care and public health.

Nursing careers are also plentiful in specialties such as informatics, education, administration and research. Nurse informaticists are in great demand for the development and implementation of clinical documentation systems. Nurse educators are needed to train new nurses to feed the overall strong demand. Nurse administrators are important to guide the work of health care, and nurse researchers are essential to contribute to our knowledge of effective health care. In this chapter, we will go into detail about the different nursing specialties.

Hospital Nursing Specialties

Many hospital specialties are available for RNs and advanced practice nurses. Typical hospital work may also occur at other sites, usually in community or long-term care. Advanced practice nurses providing hospital care include clinical nurse specialists, acute care NPs and nurse anesthetists.

Types of hospital nurses

Critical care nurses provide critical/intensive care in hospitals; patients most often have cardiovascular, respiratory or pulmonary failure.

Emergency/trauma nurses provide emergency care for life-threatening conditions due to accidents, heart attacks and strokes. Emergency nurses most often work in hospitals, in the military, or in emergency transit, such as flight nurses.

Visit Vault at **www.vault.com** for insider company profiles, expert advice, career message boards, expert resume reviews, the Vault Job Board and more.

VAULT CAREER LIBRARY   17

- **Medical-surgical nurses** are the most numerous; they care for a variety of patients in hospitals, clinics, home care and nursing homes.

- **Nurse anesthetists** are advanced practice nurses who manage anesthesia for patients undergoing surgery.

- **Perianesthesia nurses** work during surgery to care for patients under anesthesia.

- **Perioperative nurses** work inside operating rooms to assist surgeons in a variety of surgical specialties.

- **Psychiatric nurses** work with patients in hospitals and community settings who have personality and mood disorders.

- **Radiologic nurses** care for patients undergoing ultrasounds, magnetic resonance imaging and other radiologic procedures.

- **Rehabilitation nurses** take care of patients with disabilities due to a variety of events, such as hip replacement surgery, stroke and traumatic brain injury.

- **Transplant nurses** provide care for patients receiving transplants and their living donors.

- **Nurse administrators** are employed by health care facilities to supervise and manage nursing staff, maintain employee work schedules and budgets, and oversee supply inventories.

Other types of nurses

Addictions nurses care for people with alcohol, drug and tobacco addictions. Developmental disabilities nurses work with disabled people challenged by ongoing physical, mental or behavioral disabilities. Nurses may help with activities of daily living, including feeding, elimination and mobility. Diabetes management nurses work with diabetic people to teaching self-care, including nutrition, exercise, blood sugar testing, and medication and insulin administration. HIV/AIDS nurses take care of patients living with HIV and AIDS. Oncology nurses work with patients and families facing many varieties of cancer and the associated radiation and chemotherapies. Wound, ostomy and continence nurses care for patients with wounds from injury, disease or surgery; care for people with surgical openings for elimination of bodily wastes; and care for patients disabled by bowel and bladder incontinence.

Community and Public Health Care

Home health care nurses provide real or virtual visits to patients at home and support family caregivers. Patients who have insurance reimbursement for home care RN visits are most usually recovering from surgery, accidents and childbirth. Medicare reimburses home care for a period of time after a hospitalization for severe medical illness, such as congestive heart failure. Positions in home health care are predicted to rise due to the growing numbers of elderly and infirm persons with Medicare coverage. Because of the independent nature of this work, and the growing number of complex procedures performed in the home, RNs are usually required to have a year or two of work experience in a general medical-surgical floor of a hospital before employment in home health care by Visiting Nurse Services. Home health care nurses will work most usually for a nonprofit agency that provides home care subsequent to a physician's order. Public health nurses work in publicly-funded city or county health departments to provide health screenings, patient education and infectious disease control. For example, public health nurses may be in charge of screening for tuberculosis or sexually transmitted diseases and providing treatment and patient education as needed.

Ambulatory Care

Positions in outpatient practice (such as private offices and public clinics) are available for RNs and for advanced practice nurses. RNs most usually work with a physician or NP to initiate care when a patient comes to the office to triage or determine the need for immediate care, and to provide patient education. Some RNs provide patient support by telephone rather than face to face. This is especially common in pediatric offices and in some health maintenance organizations where patients are encouraged to phone for advice that may prevent or delay the need for face-to-face care. Nurses in outpatient practice, self-employed or employed by physicians, may specialize in many areas, as follows.

Types of outpatient nurses

• **Cardiac and vascular nurses** care for patients with heart disease and heart surgery. They may be involved with postoperative rehabilitation, which commonly involves blood pressure, activity and diet monitoring.

Visit Vault at **www.vault.com** for insider company profiles, expert advice, career message boards, expert resume reviews, the Vault Job Board and more.

VAULT CAREER LIBRARY

19

• **Dermatology nurses** focus on patients with skin diseases and skin cancer.

• **Gastroenterology nurses** care for people with diseases of the stomach and intestines, such as gastroesophageal reflux and inflammatory bowel syndrome. Nurses may become skilled in a variety of endoscopic procedures to examine the inside of the gastrointestinal tract with special equipment.

• **Gynecology nurses** care for women with reproductive system problems, such as cancer and sexually transmitted diseases.

• **Nurse midwives** are advanced practice nurses who care for childbearing women during the preconception, prenatal, intrapartum and postpartum periods.

• **Nephrology nurses** focus on patients with kidney disease.

• **Neuroscience nurses** work with patients with nervous system problems, such as seizures and spinal cord injuries.

• **Ophthalmic nurses** care for patients with eye disorders and eye surgery.

• **Orthopedic nurses** focus on patients with muscular and skeletal problems, including sports injuries and fractures, arthritis and joint replacement.

• **Ear-nose-throat nurses** provide care for patients with ear, nose and throat problems, including allergies, infections and congenital defects.

• **Respiratory nurses** work with patients who have respiratory problems such as asthma, chronic obstructive pulmonary disease (related to smoking), and cystic fibrosis.

• **Urology nurses** focus on patients with kidney and urinary tract problems, as well as problems with male reproductive organs.

• **Genetics nurses** work with patients and families to educate them as to available screenings for genetic disease, and treat people with genetic disorders, including sickle cell disease and cystic fibrosis.

Nurse practitioners

Nurse practitioners work as primary and specialty care providers in outpatient settings such as private offices and public clinics. NPs provide health promotion and disease prevention services, and care for people with acute and chronic diseases. NPs may provide periodic examinations and lab work to screen for common illnesses, such as hypertension and diabetes, and may manage the care for these. Many NPs work with vulnerable populations in nonprofit or publicly-funded clinics in medically underserved areas. There is a great need for bilingual NPs in many areas of the U.S. NPs may specialize in family practice, adult practice, women's health, pediatrics, acute care (adult, pediatric and neonatal), gerontology, mental health and many other subspecialties. NPs can prescribe medications in all 50 states.

Nursing Homes and Extended Care

RNs in nursing homes and extended care often are the most knowledgeable professionals on site; they supervise aides and LPNs providing direct care. They may be the top administrator in charge of the facility. Positions for RNs in nursing homes and extended care are expected to grow quite rapidly due to increasing numbers of elderly in the U.S. who are no longer able to live in their own homes. In addition, nursing homes provide rehabilitation, many times for patients discharged after a brief hospital stay for hip replacement surgery and the like. Furthermore, specialized rehabilitation in nursing homes for stroke and head injury, as well as Alzheimer's and dementia patients, is expected to increase. Assisted living facilities are becoming more prevalent; many of these are adjacent to a nursing home where patients may move when their independence declines. Often, RNs and NPs play a large role in health promotion and assessment on site.

Nursing Educators

Nurses with advanced degrees teach at college and university levels. Some nurse educators teach continuing education or orientation within hospitals. They may teach topics in general or specialty nursing. In addition, those in universities usually are expected to publish articles and develop research projects with funding from government or private foundations. Nursing faculty positions vary according to the resources of the institution. Because some universities are associated with large health science centers, clinical teaching opportunities are available on campus. However, many nursing schools are in universities without a medical school or health science center. In these schools, the clinical teaching may be widespread about the community hospitals and health care system.

In general, nursing education is very demanding due to relatively low salaries and large responsibilities in classroom and clinical teaching as well as university and professional service and the expectation to bring in funding for

Visit Vault at www.vault.com for insider company profiles, expert advice, career message boards, expert resume reviews, the Vault Job Board and more.

VAULT CAREER LIBRARY   21

research. These realities have led to a growing shortage of nursing faculty across the country. Nurses who enjoy teaching and who appreciate the self-determined schedule of academia may thrive in the role.

Other Types of Nurses

Nurses work in other settings, including schools, industry, informatics and a variety of businesses related to health care. School nurses work to ensure that students have required immunizations and health screenings. They may also provide first aid and administer daily medications to students. NPs may manage school-based clinics in many districts. These clinics often provide routine care to students and their families.

Occupational health nurses

Occupational health nurses work inside businesses to treat job-related injuries and illnesses. They work within the human resources department at the work site. They also work to prevent accidents by detecting workplace hazards and ensuring health and safety standards. Many occupational health nurses provide health education and health promotion to employees. Similarly, nurses may work in related facilities, such as correctional institutions, summer camps and the military.

Holistic nurses

Holistic nurses care for people who desire alternative care, such as acupuncture, massage and aromatherapy, and biofeedback. Holistic care is meant to encompass mental, spiritual and physical health. It is usually provided in office settings.

Case managers

Case managers are nurses who work in a variety of sites, inside or outside hospitals, with patients and their care givers to coordinate care from various sources. Case managers may work within the hospital to facilitate discharge planning and follow-up care. Or, they may work in specialty areas, such as HIV or substance abuse care in the community health center.

Forensics nurses

Forensics nurses bring nursing skills to law enforcement to both treat and investigate victims of sexual assault, child abuse or accidental death. They may work within an emergency room or in a law enforcement agency.

Infection control nurses

Infection control nurses are employed by health care facilities to investigate and prevent infectious outbreaks and to prepare to respond to biological terrorism. Most large hospitals now have infection control nurses.

Legal nurse consultants

Legal nurse consultants may be self-employed or employed by lawyers to gather evidence from patients, witnesses, and medical and billing records for medical cases.

Nurse informaticists

Nurse informaticists are employed by health care facilities or information technology companies to arrange for the collection and analysis of health care data. More and more hospitals and ambulatory offices are looking for skilled nurse informaticists to facilitate the documentation of care to examine its quality and to contain costs. RNs also may be employed by a wide variety of agencies to work as private consultants, public policy advisors, pharmaceutical researchers and salespersons, and medical writers and editors.

RNs and advanced practice nurses

Some nurses manage health care businesses in ambulatory, acute, home-based and chronic care. RNs and advanced practice nurses are in demand by employers in hospitals, insurance and pharmaceutical companies. RNs working in these business arenas may have responsibilities in many areas, including planning, marketing, policy development, quality assurance and research. For example, an experienced RN may be hired by a pharmaceutical company to manage a research study regarding the safety and effectiveness of a new drug. Or, an RN with several years' experience may work with a health insurance company or hospital to study "best practices" in health care and to train others to implement them to improve the quality of care provided.

Visit Vault at **www.vault.com** for insider company profiles, expert advice, career message boards, expert resume reviews, the Vault Job Board and more.

VAULT CAREER LIBRARY   23

Nursing Skills

All nurses must be skilled at working with people and at applying their knowledge of physiology and pathophysiology to patients' potential and actual health problems. Nursing skills include communication, physical examination, diagnosing problems, problem solving with the patient, intervening with patient education and technical procedures, coordinate care across providers and sites, and advocate for the best care for the patient.

Basic Nursing Skills

Communication

Communication is the foundation of working with people; nurses learn verbal communication skills such as reflective listening, repeating, summarizing and clarifying. Good communication facilitates relationship building with patients, families and other members of the health care team, such as physicians and other therapists. Much communication is written out to document the care given. Nurses must be able to write clearly and concisely to describe the assessment, diagnosis and plan for each patient. Nurse researchers have identified the "Nursing Minimum Data Set" with information to record on every patient encounter.

Nurses must take the information communicated by the patient and family (also known as the "history"), and information gathered by physical examination or laboratory tests and determine a diagnosis. The mental activity of making a diagnosis is to match the assessed patient problem(s), resources and goals with available treatments that are based on scientific evidence. For example, evidence-based guidelines outline routine care for diabetics that will keep their blood sugar under control and thereby decrease complications and hospitalizations. In this case, the medical diagnosis is "Diabetes Mellitus, type 2", and there may be several nursing diagnoses—a common one is knowledge deficit related to the disease process. The recommended interventions, based on research, include medications, laboratory testing and referrals, as well as teaching about the disease process, teaching foot care, teaching activity care and teaching nutrition care. Often, nursing interventions are individualized based on cultural and economic influences. The nursing process involves effective problem solving that leads

Visit Vault at **www.vault.com** for insider company profiles, expert advice, career message boards, expert resume reviews, the Vault Job Board and more.

VAULT CAREER LIBRARY   25

to a defined plan of action with interventions based on solid research evidence.

Skilled educators

Nurses must be skilled at educating patients and families. Research shows that the most frequent nursing intervention in most settings is teaching and counseling. The first step in teaching is assessment of the patient's baseline knowledge, so that time is not spent going over information that is already known. Assessment also allows for clarification and correction of any prior inaccurate information. Subsequently, education will fill in gaps in knowledge pertaining to the diagnoses, goals or plan of care. Often, nurses will teach about the normal functions of the body and how disease disrupts them. Recommended treatments can be explained in turn. In addition, after a risk assessment, nurses will teach how to prevent common problems that could complicate recovery and limit years of healthy life. One recommended principle of education is to transmit the teaching in several ways, using pictures and written materials, as well as discussion. For example, to teach a new diabetic, pictures of the pancreas and digestive organs and photos or videos of insulin injection technique will be used along with discussion and written instruction. Nowadays, multimedia and Internet-based presentations are often available for common problems. One evolving aspect of patient education, considered to be a feature of informatics used by all nurses, is for the nurse to evaluate educational materials and direct patients and families to the most up-to-date and accurate sources.

Skills usually identified with nursing tend to be those referred to as procedural or technical. This includes insertion of intravenous (IV) catheters, placement and reading of electrocardiograms (ECG), injecting vaccines and medications, and wound care. Most technical skills are done by several different types of professionals and the specific skills needed are matched to a certain work environment. For example, NPs in outpatient practice do not routinely insert IVs, but RNs in hospitals do. ECGs are often read by physicians, but RNs in critical care are very skilled in their reading. Medications may be injected by patients themselves and by all types of health care providers. The general preparation that an RN receives in a bachelor's program will give an introduction to many commonly used procedures such as those just mentioned, but further on-the-job training is needed to build proficiency for most of these. That is one reason behind the requirement of a year or so of work experience before entrance to most advanced practice master's programs in critical care or neonatal care.

Case management

Care coordination, or case management, is one of the most important nursing skills for today's complex environment in health care. Many different health care professionals may be involved in this function, but because of their close and frequent patient contact in all health care settings, nurses often take the lead role. Depending on the problems the patient faces, there may be a need for a myriad of health care services, such as social work, medical equipment, medications, transportation, legal advice, housing, nutrition support, housekeeping support, safety and communications support, etc. Nurses are often in a position to serve as "command central" to coordinate these services to preserve and restore health. Indeed, a required part of planning a hospital discharge is to assess the resources and environment where the patient is going next.

Advocacy

Advocacy is a nursing skill useful on both micro and macro levels. An individual patient may benefit from nursing advocacy when, for example, he has no health insurance and little cash to purchase a medication prescribed by a physician. The nurse, knowing the relative costs of equally effective medications, could approach the physician and advocate for a less expensive prescription. On the macro level, nurses belong to professional organizations, such as the American Nurses Association (ANA), which maintain lobbyists to speak up for legislation to benefit the health of all Americans. ANA lobbyists also speak in favor of specific measures to benefit the profession of nursing, such as funding for collegiate nursing education, and state and federal laws pertaining to the licensure of foreign-trained nurses. Over the years, nursing advocacy has been key in making birth control legal and available and improving the health of low-income and vulnerable families.

Clinical Nursing Duties

Nurses learn to step through a consistent and deliberate process of gathering information and solving problems to provide care. This same process is used in all specialties, including those without direct patient care (such as informatics, administration and education). Each bit of pertinent information is recorded for future reference. The documentation may be done on paper or entered into an electronic health record. The patient record is a legal document, owned by the patient and the provider who recorded it, governed

Visit Vault at **www.vault.com** for insider company profiles, expert advice, career message boards, expert resume reviews, the Vault Job Board and more.

VAULT CAREER LIBRARY   **27**

by federal privacy laws (HIPAA), and subject to legal review in situations such as insurance oversight and alleged malpractice or negligence.

One prominent nurse researcher has found that over time, nurses progress in stages of growth, beginning as a novice, moving to an advanced beginner, to a competent practitioner, to a proficient clinician, and finally to a skilled, expert nurse. The expert nurse has developed tremendous perceptual ability and common sense about patient assessment and care, going beyond tasks to respond to the whole patient and family situation. For example, an expert nurse with years of experience caring for asthma will quickly assess an asthmatic child's breathing condition and treatment history, as well as the family's financial ability to purchase needed medications, and knowledge of when to use specific medications. All of these factors are essential in asthma management.

The patient history

In gathering the history, a nurse will first identify the chief complaint or the problem at hand by asking the patient, family or previous provider. To clarify the history of present illness, questions are asked about symptoms. These questions will establish a description of the symptoms, including the onset, location, duration and what has helped or made symptoms worse. To get to know the patient and ascertain health risk factors, background information will be obtained from interviews or records. The background, or patient history, includes information about the past and present such as: What was your education? Where did you grow up? Where do you live? Who do you live with? What do you do in a typical day and typical week? What did you eat, drink and smoke in the past 24 hours? Is this typical? What exercise did you get in the past 24 hours and past week? What serious illnesses or surgeries have you had? What serious diseases have your immediate family members had? What medications, vitamins and herbs do you take regularly?

Usually, the history is very comprehensive as the patient begins care. Later on, the nurse's questions may be tailored to the chief complaint and the specialty of care; often the history is rather brief and specific. A paper or electronic checklist or outline is often used to enhance speed and thoroughness. When the patient's history is recorded electronically in a structured way, it may be readily accessed to group with other similar patients. For example, an outbreak of a contagious illness, such as influenza, may be located by public health nurse surveillance of data from patients' symptoms in local emergency rooms. This capacity to aggregate, or group data, is one of the strengths of informatics.

The physical exam

Another component of assessment is the physical exam. Nurses measure the patient's height and weight and vital signs, including blood pressure, temperature, pulse and respirations. Then an examination of body systems will be done, pertaining to the chief complaint and the role of the nurse involved in the care. For example, a primary care nurse practitioner may perform a rather complete physical exam of the entire body for a newborn or a periodic health maintenance exam. A medical-surgical nurse caring for a patient hospitalized with congestive heart failure may listen to the heart and lungs, check the legs for swelling, and observe the amount of fluid input and output. A nurse visiting a homebound patient recovering from surgery may check the wound for redness, swelling and healing as she changes the dressing and asks the patient about pain management.

Lab tests

Also within an assessment are laboratory and radiology data. Nurse practitioners commonly order all types of lab and radiology tests pertinent to determining a diagnosis or managing a disease. Depending on state law and the rules in the workplace, NPs are authorized to order labs, X-rays, MRIs, ultrasounds, etc. Registered nurses (RN) often work under a physician's standing orders to administer lab tests, such as urinalysis and urine pregnancy tests, in defined situations. Standing orders are written by a physician to legally cover an RN who decides to administer a listed lab test or medication when the situation calls for it. For example, there may be a standing order for the RN to administer a urinalysis for each pregnant woman who comes for a checkup. There may be a standing order for the RN to administer measles, mumps and rubella vaccines to each child over one year of age. (It is worth noting here that licensed practical nurses, LPNs, often are called upon to administer standing orders from a physician, NP or an RN. Legally, only an RN may receive orders from an NP or physician. This is because each order should be verified and checked for accuracy and the one-year LPN education is limited in this regard. LPNs are licensed to work under the supervision of an RN, advanced practice nurse—such as an NP, or a physician.)

Diagnosis

Once the assessment is done, the nurse uses his experience and education to determine the patient's problem(s), also known as nursing diagnoses. Assessing and diagnosing may be iterative or back-and-forth, where once a

Visit Vault at **www.vault.com** for insider company profiles, expert advice, career message boards, expert resume reviews, the Vault Job Board and more.

VAULT CAREER LIBRARY 29

preliminary diagnosis is made, more assessment by the nurse may refine or change the diagnosis. This is especially necessary in intensive care where the patient's condition changes continuously. Nursing diagnoses are usually combined with medical disease diagnoses. Nursing diagnoses may be disease-related, but can also often directly refer to the patient's experience. For example, a nurse may diagnose "inconsistent medication administration" in conjunction with a medical diagnosis of "hypertension."

Based on the diagnoses, goals for care are determined in concert with the patient and family and a plan is made. Goals are based on current evidence regarding effective and available treatments, and are tailored according to the patient's culture and informed consent. Generally, a great deal of patient and family education must take place to ensure informed consent. Nurses should excel at exploring the patient's and family's baseline knowledge on a topic and adding essential pieces to that knowledge. Nowadays, many patients have gone to the Internet to research their concerns, and may need clarification and guidance from their nurse regarding further questions.

Plan of care

The plan of care varies according to the patient's desires and the specialty of the nurse. For example, an RN's plan for an adult hospitalized in a medical-surgical unit will most likely include physician's orders to administer medications or procedures as well as care initiated by the nurse, such as assessing skin integrity and turning every two hours to prevent skin breakdown ("bedsores"). An NP's plan for a child with diabetes might include a prescription for medication (as stated earlier, NPs can prescribe in all 50 states), parent or caretaker education regarding administering the medication at home, and a referral to a dietician for complex nutrition problems that are identified. A CNM's plan for a pregnant woman might include orders for a panel of blood and other laboratory tests, patient education regarding signs and symptoms of labor onset and a referral to WIC, the federal nutrition program for women, infants and children. A CRNA's plan for an anesthetized man might well include the administration of anesthesia and oxygen, and the constant monitoring of blood pressure and cardiac function. A CNS's plan for a hospitalized patient might include patient education regarding a living will, an order for a psychology consult and a referral to a social worker to set up nursing home placement upon discharge. A DNP's plan for a patient in long-term care might include a referral for physical therapy and occupational therapy rehabilitation, and education of the family regarding how to provide a safe environment and manage care and follow-up upon discharge.

Each nurse will intervene by executing the plan. In an environment with 24/7 care, such as a hospital or nursing home, it is important to have a group of nurses involved with each patient. Often, there is a primary nurse identified as the leader of an individual patient's care. In outpatient and home care, care is attributed to an individual nurse for billing purposes. The nurse will evaluate the care given and reassess the patient to determine the outcomes of care and to adjust the goals and plan as needed.

The Nursing Minimum Data Set

Because written communication is so important in providing care and keeping a legal record, and because computers are used to record information, the Nursing Minimum Data Set has become more prominent in the U.S. and internationally. It is the foundation of accurate nursing documentation for individual care and also for aggregate data showing what nurses do. It is the basis for the specialty of nursing informatics. The Nursing Minimum Data Set includes:

NURSING CARE ELEMENTS

• Nursing diagnosis
• Nursing intervention
• Nursing outcome
• Nursing intensity (a measure of work effort)

CLIENT ELEMENTS

• Unique individual identifier number
• Date of birth
• Gender
• Race and ethnicity
• Residence

SERVICE PROVIDER ELEMENTS

• Unique facility identifier
• Unique health record number
• Unique health provider identifier
• Encounter date
• Discharge date
• Disposition of client
• Expected payer of bill

Visit Vault at **www.vault.com** for insider company profiles, expert advice, career message boards, expert resume reviews, the Vault Job Board and more.

VAULT CAREER LIBRARY

31

With the advent of computerized documentation, nurses recording data must use standardized terminology that the computer will recognize and be able to group or aggregate to generate statistics to evaluate patient outcomes, effective performance of health care providers, monitor patient safety and conduct other types of research. Standardized terminologies contain a number code that the computer recognizes linked with text that humans recognize. (Usually, nurses do not have to remember the number codes.)

Minimum Data Set structure

More and more nursing documentation is structured into easy checkboxes or limited lists of terms and may be in a computerized template within an electronic patient record. An example follows—a brief check list of patient teaching and counseling that was used in a small handheld computer by FNP students to document the primary care they provided in conjunction with encounters for common medical and nursing diagnoses (such as hypertension, well child care or knowledge deficit regarding the disease process). These nursing interventions are taken from a longer list in the Clinical Care Classification terminology (see www.sabacare.com). The data collected by the students were analyzed to determine which interventions were related to which patient demographics and which diagnoses. Students then kept a portfolio of their own clinical experiences and faculty examined the group's accomplishments. The results showed that students were following national research-based guidelines for care.

CODE	TEXT	CHECK if applicable
A01.03	Activity Care	
A04.03	Sleep Pattern Control	
B06.03	Bowel Care	
T58.03	Bladder Care	
F15.13	Hydration Control	
Q49.03	Ear Care	
Q50.03	Eye Care	
R53.03	Mouth Care	
R54.03	Skin Care	
S56.03	Foot Care	
M39.13	Home Situation Analysis	
E12.13	Coping Support	
Z03.03	Caregiver Coping Support	

CODE	TEXT	CHECK if applicable
Z05.03	Parenting	
D10.03	Behavior Care	
D11.03	Reality Orientation	
N68.03	Violence Control	
N41.03	Emergency Care	
N42.03	Safety Precautions	
Z01.13	Disease Process	
G18.63	Compliance with Therapeutic Regimen	
G19.23	Nursing Care Coordination	
H24.33	Medication Side Effects	
H24.13	Medication Actions	
J29.03	Nutrition Care	
J66.03	Breastfeeding Support	
G18.13	Compliance with Diet	
Q47.03	Pain Control	
K31.23	Health Promotion	
N40.03	Substance Abuse Control	
N40.13	Tobacco Abuse Control	
N40.23	Alcohol Abuse Control	
U74.03	Reproductive Care	
U76.03	Growth & Development Care	
U76.13	Newborn Care (First 30 D)	
U76.23	Infant Care (31 D-11 M)	
U76.33	Child Care (1-11 Y)	
U76.43	Adolescent Care (12-20 Y)	
U76.53	Adult Care (21-64 Y)	
U76.63	Older Adult Care (= > 65 Y)	
L36.03	Pulmonary Care	
I27.03	Diabetic Care	
K30.03	Infection Control	
Z04.03	STD Control	
Z06.03	Pre/Post-Operative Care	
E14.23	Dying/Death Measures	
G19.13	Bill of Rights	

Visit Vault at **www.vault.com** for insider company profiles, expert advice,
career message boards, expert resume reviews, the Vault Job Board and more.

VAULT CAREER LIBRARY   33

Code of Ethics

Nurses are responsible and accountable, both ethically and legally, for the patient care they provide. They work to promote health, prevent illness, restore health and alleviate suffering. According to the International Council of Nursing, there are four principal elements of ethical nursing conduct. These are: (1) responsibility to people and their rights; (2) personal responsibility and accountability for safe practice and continuing competence; (3) professional standards for evidence-based practice, management, education and research; and (4) safe and cooperative work with others. Because of a long history of ethical behavior, nurses are highly respected and trusted by the public.

Quality control

Currently, many institutions and payers oversee quality care outcome evaluations. In hospitals and health care organizations accredited by JCAHO (Joint Commission on Accreditation of Healthcare Organizations, "Jayco"), outcome evaluations are known as performance measurements and are targeted to high-cost and high-risk practices such as treatments for heart failure, heart attack, heart surgery and pneumonia. Patient safety goals have been set by JCAHO to prevent dangerous conditions (such as errors in medication dosage) during treatment.

Medicare, the federal government's health insurance plan for disabled Americans and all Americans over age 65, is moving toward "pay for performance" where incentive payments with Medicare reimbursement to NPs and physicians will be offered when care for common chronic diseases is evaluated to meet national evidence-based guidelines. These diseases include coronary artery disease, diabetes and heart failure.

Looking forward

In the coming years, more individual patient data on assessment, diagnosis, interventions and outcomes will be entered into computers for use by health care organizations, making the work of quality evaluation and outcome research much more efficient. It is essential that computerized patient care data include the work of nurses as well as physicians and other members of the health care team. Nurses usually think of individual patients one by one as they work with them. Outcomes for individuals are certainly very important. However, outcomes for groups of people with similar diagnoses and similar treatments can be generated by computerized data. This will be a powerful tool to reveal evidence on what works in health care. At present, the majority of health care treatments by nurses and physicians are not supported by strong research. With a few years of computerized outcome data on hundreds and thousands of patients, we may be more adept at using scarce resources in ways that will really make a difference. Many nurse researchers and nurse informatics specialists are working to make this happen.

Visit Vault at **www.vault.com** for insider company profiles, expert advice, career message boards, expert resume reviews, the Vault Job Board and more.

VAULT CAREER LIBRARY

35

GETTING HIRED

Education

Nursing responsibilities are often life-sustaining. Nurses must be very conscientious, caring and careful with detail. Nurses are responsible for patient assessment and knowing when to institute nursing care and when to consult with other providers. Many nurses supervise others working with patients. As Florence Nightingale pointed out, nurses must arrange for care to continue in their absence. Nurses need to have emotional control and emotional stability to cope with patient and family suffering, emergencies and disasters. You will want to feature these important skills in your education and job application.

Hands-On Training

Nursing education includes both classroom theory instruction and hands-on, supervised clinical experience in hospitals and health care facilities. Course work includes anatomy, physiology, microbiology, chemistry, nutrition, psychology and behavioral sciences, liberal arts courses and nursing.

Clinical experience in a variety of settings is provided, depending on the nursing specialty. The generalist BSN nurse will have clinical experience in various hospital areas, including medical-surgical, pediatrics, maternity, emergency, psychiatry and operating/recovery room. Experience in community and home health, as well as long-term care and ambulatory care is also included.

Nursing Degrees

Education for nurses at the baccalaureate, master's and doctoral levels includes the study of anatomy, physiology, genetics, microbiology, pharmacology and therapeutics, psychology, sociology, ethics, policy and research.

Bachelor's degree

A bachelor's degree, rather than an associate's degree, in nursing is highly recommended. Career and educational advancement are severely limited for a nurse with an associate's degree. Administrative positions require a bachelor's degree. Because the BSN includes four full years of collegiate education, students receive more science background and more experience in communication skills, leadership and critical thinking, as well as more non-hospital clinical experience.

A BSN is required for graduate education and national certification in advanced practice in all specialties—nurse practitioner, clinical nurse specialist, nurse anesthetist and nurse midwife. In addition, graduate education is needed for positions in teaching, research, consulting and management. More and more schools are offering accelerated BSN programs, for people with a bachelor's degree not in nursing who want to pursue a graduate degree in nursing. In 2004, 46 schools offered accelerated BSN-to-doctoral programs for individuals who want to do nursing research and teach nursing.

Over 250 bachelor's degree programs in nursing are accredited by the National League for Nursing Accrediting Commission and/or the Commission on Collegiate Nursing Education. Each of these accrediting organizations also accredits master's and doctoral programs. Each has a web site listing the programs they currently endorse.

Master's degree

In 2004, 417 nursing schools offered master's degrees and 93 offered doctoral degrees. Only 13 percent of RNs in 2004 held a master's or doctoral degree. The demand for nurses with graduate degrees is extreme now and is projected to grow tremendously due to cost pressures limiting physician education and practice and due to the forecasted continuing need to educate more nurses. These highly educated nurses are needed both to provide expert care and to teach the next generation of nurses. Graduate degrees in nursing include a Master of Science in Nursing (MSN), a Doctor of Nursing Practice (DNP or DrNP), a Doctor of Nursing Science (DNS or DNSc), and a Doctor of Philosophy (PhD). For advanced clinical practice, an MSN or DNP is required. For research and teaching at the university level, a DNS or PhD is required. The number of schools offering the DNP is growing, due to the recognition that NPs will benefit from additional courses in quality assessment and evidence-based practice. Schools with a DNS offer that research degree through the school or college of nursing itself, in contrast to the PhD, which meets full university approval and standards to be offered through the university. Many DNS programs have evolved into PhD programs, after full university review and approval.

Some schools offer a joint MSN and MPH (master's in public health) or MBA (master's in business administration). These joint degrees may be of interest if you plan to use both the nursing and the related field of knowledge in your work. For example, a hospital administrator may find the MSN/MBA useful; an international health worker may find the MSN/MPH useful. Often the joint degree programs, as the accelerated BSN/MSN programs, will allow overlap so that one course "counts" for both degrees. Therefore, your time in school and your tuition costs are minimized.

Cost

Nursing education is available at many public and private universities. Usually, the first year of study includes basic science courses, such as biology and anatomy, that may be transferred if the university where you begin does not have a nursing degree. Top schools for nursing degrees are published annually by *U.S. News & World Report*. The rankings are determined by faculty surveys and research funding, and are somewhat controversial. In general, if the university as a whole has a good reputation for quality, the undergraduate nursing program will be strong.

According to the College Board, the annual tuition costs for a four-year degree ranges from an average of $5,836 for a public university to an average of $13,200 for private universities. Many scholarships are available for undergraduate study, including federal Pell grants and Stafford and Perkins loans.

Financial aid for graduate study in nursing, as in other fields, is most likely to involve loans, rather than scholarships   However, some employers, such as hospitals and universities, provide tuition assistance for graduate study. In addition, the federal government sponsors traineeships through the Division of Nursing directly to selected nursing schools that notify students of their federal tuition assistance. In addition, the federal National Health Service Corps scholarships and loan repayment is available for family and pediatric nurse practitioners who pay back by working in an underserved area for a period of time after graduation. At the doctoral level, many schools that offer a PhD are committed to full tuition support for full-time students through teaching assistantships and research assistantships. Doctoral students select courses or research projects to assist with and receive tuition plus a modest monthly stipend.

Visit Vault at **www.vault.com** for insider company profiles, expert advice, career message boards, expert resume reviews, the Vault Job Board and more.

VAULT CAREER LIBRARY   **41**

Distance Education

Distance education is growing and currently is available at all levels of nursing education. It has pros and cons for each student and for the profession as a whole.

On the plus side, it can fit into a busy lifestyle, it has few geographic limitations and it fosters independent study. But supervision of hands-on clinical experience is difficult, there is a lack of live group interaction and support, and it requires technology resources that everyone may not have access to.

It may be that a hybrid with some aspects of distance Internet course work and a period of live interaction and clinical skill assessment may best serve aspiring nurses. The application of distance education is being tested in many disciplines such as business and the sciences. In nursing, it is important to include a strong clinical component with appropriate oversight.

Licensing/Certification

Each professional nurse is licensed by the state and is accountable for her own autonomous practice. Nurses practice within ethical and legal standards to provide safe, state-of-the-art care. According to the International Council of Nurses, professional ethics are applied to nursing practice. Nurses must respect the right of each individual to determine his or her own care. Legal mandates for nurses come from state laws and licensing acts. Nurses are legally mandated to report child and elder abuse to the appropriate state agency and to obtain emergency care for a person who is in danger of harming himself or others.

In order to obtain a state license as a registered nurse, all nursing graduates must graduate from a program approved by that state, and pass a national licensing examination, known as the NCLEX-RN—a written exam that covers all types of nursing situations (see www.ncsbn.org). The NCLEX-RN test questions are carefully developed and revised each year to evaluate fundamental, entry-level nursing practice knowledge and behaviors. To develop the test, the activities of newly licensed nurses were analyzed regarding their frequency, their location and their impact on patient safety. The National Council of State Boards of Nursing maintains a list of each of their state board members; the individual states have a list of approved nursing educational programs and can inform you of dates and locations to take the NCLEX-RN exam. Each undergraduate nursing school has information about the percentage of their graduates that pass the NCLEX-RN exam each year.

The pass rate for BSNs educated in the U.S. and taking the test for the first time in 2006 was 88.1 percent. The pass rate for RNs educated outside of the U.S. and taking the test for the first time in 2006 was 61.2 percent.

The NCLEX exam provides a "floor" of competency for safe nursing practice. It is a computer adaptive test; each test is interactively developed based on the candidates' responses to the questions, so it is not too hard or too easy, but adapted to your ability level. You'll have a maximum of six hours to take the test; you will answer a minimum of 75 and a maximum of 265 questions, including 15 experimental questions that are being tried out for a new test. Every question counts. The questions, which involve integrated nursing content, are written to go beyond memorization and recall to application and analysis of information. NCLEX study books are widely available to prepare for the exam. Many online study guides and practice tests are available for a fee.

NCLEX Blueprint:

Client needs

1. Safe and effective care environment

    a. Management of care (13-19% of questions)
    b. Safety and infection control (8-14% of questions)

2. Health promotion and maintenance (6-12% of questions)

3. Psychosocial integrity (6-12% of questions)

4. Physiological integrity

    a. Basic care and comfort (6-12%)
    b. Pharmacological and parenteral therapies (13-19%)
    c. Reduction of risk potential (13-19%)
    d. Physiological adaptation (11-17%)

Nurses may be licensed in more than one state. An endorsement process is undertaken to get practice privileges in additional states. Currently 18 states are members of the Nurse Licensure Compact Agreement, which allows nurses to practice in each of these states. Periodic license renewal is necessary in all states, and may require evidence of continuing education.

Visit Vault at **www.vault.com** for insider company profiles, expert advice, career message boards, expert resume reviews, the Vault Job Board and more.

VAULT CAREER LIBRARY   **43**

Several professional organizations certify advanced practice nurses with a master's degree, depending on the specialty. These include the American Association of Nurse Anesthetists, the American College of Nurse Midwives, the American Nurses Credentialing Center and others. See the Appendix for a list of certifying organizations and their web sites. Increasingly, and in many states, national specialty certification is required in order to practice.

The Hiring Process

With the right education, it's time to apply for a job. In this chapter, we will discuss the basics of beginning your career as a nurse, such as where to apply and resume, cover letter and interview advice.

Where to Apply

There are five major employment settings for nurses: hospitals, which employ half of all nurses; community and public health settings (such as home care and city or county health departments); ambulatory care settings (such as private offices and walk-in clinics); nursing homes and extended care facilities; and nursing education and teaching. Other employment settings include government administration and industry (such as insurance or pharmaceutical companies).

In May 2004, the median income of registered nurses was $52,330 per year. Half of all RNs earned between $43,370 and $63,360. Annual earnings ranged from less than $37,300 to more than $74,760. The following table shows median annual earnings in several settings where the largest numbers of registered nurses worked in May 2004:

Employment services	$63,170
General medical and surgical hospitals	$53,450
Home health care services	$48,990
Offices of physicians	$48,250
Nursing care facilities	$48,220

from bhpr.hrsa.gov/healthworkforce/reports/nursing/samplesurvey04preliminary/default.htm

Information about job openings is available from personal contacts (including your clinical placements and Internet networks), in school career placement services, advertisements in print and on the Internet, state and federal employment offices, professional associations and journals, employment agencies and career consultants. Job search tips are available at stats.bls.gov/oco/oco2004.htm.

Cover Letter and Resume Advice

Cover letter

A cover letter is your introduction to the employer, and a statement of how your skills fit the position and why you would like the job. A good cover letter should be tailored to the position offered and no more than one page long. Three paragraphs are usually sufficient.

• The letter should be addressed to a specific person.

• The first paragraph should be an introduction to express your interest in the position and why you are an excellent candidate. State where you saw the position advertised. Then focus on the skills you have that the company is looking for.

• The second paragraph should elaborate on your skills and qualifications related to the particular job skills mentioned in the ad.

• The last paragraph should state that you look forward to an interview with the contact person to discuss your experiences and qualifications. Give your contact information and state that you have attached your resume to the letter. Close with: "Thank you for your attention and consideration."

Newly Graduated Nurse

555 University Ave.
Our Town, USA 12345
(222)333-4444
newnurse@gmail.com
April 15, 200X

Sally Admin, PhD, RN
Director of Nursing
Good Samaritan Hospital
Our Town, USA

Dear Dr. Admin,

I am interested in the position you advertised in the *Our Town Gazette* for a medical-surgical nurse at Good Samaritan Hospital. I will graduate with a Bachelor of Science degree in Nursing from Southern State University in May and I expect to take my NCLEX-RN licensure exam the following week. I enjoy working with medical-surgical patients. One of my clinical rotations was in Good Samaritan Hospital on Unit 9 AB. I would like to join the conscientious team of nurses that I met. I found that excellent care was provided and the nursing staff was well satisfied with the administration and the work environment.

I have a special interest in diabetes care and patient education for diabetes. While I was in nursing school, I worked for two years as a nurse's aide in Haven Health Center. Many of our patients had diabetes. I also presented a poster on Internet resources for diabetes education at our school's research day.

I look forward to an interview with you to discuss my education and experience. Please contact me at (222) 333-4444 or at the address above. I have enclosed a copy of my resume with this letter. Thank you for your attention and consideration.

Sincerely,

Newly Graduated Nurse

Visit Vault at **www.vault.com** for insider company profiles, expert advice, career message boards, expert resume reviews, the Vault Job Board and more.

VAULT CAREER LIBRARY   47

Experienced Nurse

377 College Ave.
Our Town, USA 12345
(222) 789-1011
experiencednurse@gmail.com
April 15, 200X

Sally Admin, PhD, RN
Director of Nursing
Good Samaritan Hospital
Our Town, USA

Dear Dr. Admin,

I am interested in the position you advertised in the *Our Town Gazette* for a supervising medical-surgical nurse at Good Samaritan Hospital. I have a Bachelor of Science degree in Nursing from Southern State University and six years of experience as an RN. I previously worked for three years in Good Samaritan Hospital on Unit 9 AB. I found the nurses at Good Samaritan to be very conscientious and up-to-date in providing excellent care. The nursing staff was well satisfied with the administration and the work environment. For the past three years, I have been working part time with the Visiting Nurse Service in Our Town, USA.

My nursing experience has been well rounded and has prepared me to move to a supervisory level. I understand the challenges of inpatient care and discharge planning due to the work I have done. I am well versed in most illnesses and post-surgical care and I have a special interest in diabetes. I recently presented a poster on diabetes education for families.

I look forward to an interview with you to discuss my education and experience. Please contact me at (222) 789-1011 or at the address above. I have enclosed a copy of my resume with this letter. I will be happy to provide references upon request. Thank you for your kind attention and consideration.

Sincerely,

Experienced Nurse

Resume

Your resume should be accurate and easy to read. Use a plain black font on high-quality white paper and proofread the document before you send it.

Put your name, address, e-mail and telephone number at the top. Tailor your resume to fit the job announcement. List your education, including school name and address, dates of attendance, major and highest grade completed or degree awarded. You may want to list courses or areas of focus relevant to the position. List certifications and licenses, including their numbers.

List your prior work experience (including student preceptorships and relevant volunteer work). For each job, include the job title, name and location of employer, dates of employment and a brief description of your job duties.

Highlight advanced or supervisory responsibilities and special skills, including computer skills, second language proficiency and honors.

Visit Vault at **www.vault.com** for insider company profiles, expert advice, career message boards, expert resume reviews, the Vault Job Board and more.

VAULT CAREER LIBRARY   **49**

Sample Resumes—Newly Graduated Nurse

Newly Graduated Nurse
555 University Ave.
Our Town, USA 12345
newnurse@gmail.com
(222) 333-4444

Will take the Registered Nurse NCLEX-RN exam on 5/20/0X

EDUCATION

200X	BSN, Southern State University, Our Town, USA
2000	High School Diploma, Southern High, Our Town, USA

CLINICAL ROTATIONS:

• Medical-Surgical and Pediatric at Good Samaritan Hospital in Our Town, USA
• Obstetric-Gynecological at Southern Cross Hospital in South Springfield, USA
• Psychiatric at High Hill Hospital in South Springfield, USA
• Home care at Visiting Nurse Service in Our Town, USA

SKILLS:

• Fluent in English. Eight years of Spanish study (ages 11-18 and currently studying).

• Proficient in MS Word, Excel, Powerpoint. Working knowledge of Access tables and queries. Working knowledge of Big Name Electronic Health Records.

WORK EXPERIENCE:

2003-Present   *Nurse's Aide*
                              Haven Health Care, Our Town, USA
              Nursing home care for elderly Alzheimer's patients.

2002-2003   *Waitress*
                              Salad Garden Café, Our Town, USA

2003-2004   *Volunteer*
              American Red Cross Disaster Training, Our Town, USA
                   Assisted in continuing education for professionals.

Sample Resumes—Experienced Nurse

Experienced Nurse
377 College Ave.
Our Town, USA 12345
experiencednurse@gmail.com
(222) 789-1011

Southern State RN license # 3344478

Malpractice insurance through Corporate Coverage Company

EDUCATION

2000	BSN, Southern State University, Our Town, USA

HONORS:

Graduated magna cum laude

SKILLS:

Fluent in English. Eight years of Spanish study (ages 11-18 and currently studying).

Proficient in MS Word, Excel, Powerpoint. Working knowledge of Access tables and queries. Working knowledge of Big Name Electronic Health Records.

CLINICAL EXPERIENCE:

2003-200X	**RN**
	Visiting Nurse Service, Our Town, USA
	Home visits to post-surgical and elderly patients.
2000-2003	**RN**
	Good Samaritan Hospital, Our Town, USA
	Medical-Surgical and Recovery Room
1997-2000	**Nurse's Aide**
	Haven Health Care, Our Town, USA
	Nursing home care for elderly Alzheimer's patients.

PRESENTATIONS:

2004 Poster presentation on Caring for Diabetics After Surgery: What the Family Needs to Know, Southern State Nurses' Association Annual Conference, South Springfield, USA

Visit Vault at **www.vault.com** for insider company profiles, expert advice, career message boards, expert resume reviews, the Vault Job Board and more.

VAULT CAREER LIBRARY   51

The Interview

Your interview will be your introduction and opportunity to advertise yourself and your qualifications to an employer, so be prepared! The general interview process is similar for any position in nursing. Educate yourself about the organization. Much information is available online regarding news reports about the organization, its standing in terms of quality of care, its reputation, etc. (See below in the job offer section for more ideas about researching the organization.)

Have a specific job or jobs in mind. Will you accept any schedule available? Review your resume and your qualifications for the job.

Prepare answers to general questions about your education and experience. Be prepared to discuss your school-related clinical experiences. Typical questions might require you to describe your strengths and weaknesses as well as your career goals. Practice an interview with a friend or relative.

On the day of the interview, arrive early. Be well groomed and dress appropriately. Do not chew gum or smoke. During the interview, be friendly and courteous, address the interviewer by name, speak clearly and avoid slang. Do your best to be cooperative, enthusiastic and relaxed.

Discuss why you want the position. Relate your experience in nursing school to reasons you are interested in this particular position. If you are an experienced nurse, describe your previous experience and how it will add to your expertise for the position for which you are interviewing. It helps to use body language to show interest by eye contact and leaning forward.

And do your research. Ask pertinent questions about the position but show that you have basic information about the organization from the company web site. Thank the interviewer when you leave and, as a follow-up, in writing.

Things to bring to an interview

- Social Security card.
- Government-issued identification (such as a driver's license or passport).
- Your NCLEX score, or the date you will be taking the NCLEX.
- Your RN license.
- Your malpractice insurance policy.
- Your resume. If you are applying for a teaching position, you will, instead, bring a C.V., or curriculum vitae, that includes your academic experience, publications, research and grant support, and professional/community/academic service.

On follow-up, employers may ask for references and transcripts. Contact your reference people to get permission to use them. You may want to prepare this ahead of time by requesting reference letters from nursing school faculty and from previous employers and colleagues.

Official transcripts may be required and should be ordered from the school where your degrees were awarded.

Some suggested questions

In which area is the position? What is the number of patients in this area? What is the number of nurses on each shift? How many patients would I be responsible for? What is the acuity level? What is the average length of stay for the patients? What is the turnover rate for the nurses?

If a teaching position, ask: how many courses will I teach per semester? How many student advisees will I have? How many faculty committees will I be expected to attend?

— Who is the nurse manager for the area? May I meet her before accepting the position?

— Consider specific questions regarding procedures and care related to a specialty area. For example, what nursing care standards are based on research guidelines? Is the baby "rooming in" with the mother in the postpartum area? Are pressure-equalizing mattresses used routinely post surgery? What is being done to decrease patient falls and hospital-acquired infections?

— Of what does the orientation consist? (How long? Classroom plus clinical? Mentoring?) What continuing education is available?

— Do the staff nurses belong to a labor union? Which one?

Visit Vault at **www.vault.com** for insider company profiles, expert advice, career message boards, expert resume reviews, the Vault Job Board and more.

VAULT CAREER LIBRARY   53

— How is information technology used in the institution? What patient information is available on computer? Are nursing notes documented electronically? What is the computer and Internet access for nurses to obtain reference materials and decision support?

Unless the employer initiates the subject, usually questions about salary and benefits wait for the second interview. Then you can get specifics about hourly wages, overtime, holiday pay, medical and dental insurance, life insurance, continuing education and tuition support, malpractice, etc. Most entry-level RN positions offer an hourly wage that may be higher for evening (3 to 11 p.m.) and night (11 p.m. to 7 a.m.) shifts. Most full-time positions are based on eight-hour shifts in a 35- to 40-hour week, although some may have schedules based on 12-hour schedules. Some hospitals and nursing homes offer a schedule of three 12-hour shifts per week as full time.

The Job Offer

When you receive a job offer, consider it carefully. Many times an offer is made verbally, but the job title, salary and starting date are not firm until they are in writing. Even after a written offer, you can negotiate the terms of the offer if you like. When considering an offer, it is important to imagine yourself in the environment and the specific position you will have. Think about the responsibilities you are likely to have day to day and whether these might change over time, to advance your career. Consider the potential work schedule and how that fits with your personal life and preferences. Do some research on the Internet and asking around to see if the salary and benefits offered are fair. Remember that cost of living varies a great deal in different parts of the country, as do housing and transportation costs.

Background information on an organization may come from its web site or its public relations office. Find out about its location, available transportation and parking, its age and size. If the company is publicly owned, its annual report to the stockholders discusses its mission and philosophy, history, products or services, goals and financial status. Most public/government and not-for-profit agencies also have an annual report of some type to describe their programs and missions. Ask the interviewer for names of current or former employees that you might speak to. It is interesting to find out how long people stay with the organization and how much turnover it has. It is also important to know about opportunities for advancement and promotion. Your school's career center may have additional information on employers that recruit through them.

Think about you

Consider how the size and other characteristics of the organization fit with your goals. Large organizations may offer a variety of training programs and more managerial levels for advancement, though they tend to have more specialized positions. They may offer better employee benefits than small firms. In a small organization, you may find more authority and responsibility and a closer working relationship with management. A new business may be more vulnerable to failure than an old one; yet, it may also have a potential for growth. Publicly owned and not-for-profit companies are usually governed by a board of directors so jobs are open to the most qualified people. In contrast, privately owned companies may be controlled by an individual or family who reserves the best jobs for friends and relatives.

Many companies will not discuss salary and benefits until they have decided to hire you. You will need to have an idea of the range of pay in similar jobs. This information should be available in the same places you found information about the organization. The U.S. Bureau of Labor Statistics has periodic surveys of various occupations around the country. Help-wanted ads in newspapers sometimes give salary ranges for similar positions. Remember that salary and benefits vary by geographic region, depending on differences in the cost of living. Also be aware that employers sometimes pay only a portion of benefits such as health, dental and life insurance. Employees may pay a percentage.

You need to know about your schedule and the policy regarding overtime. Find out how many hours you will be expected to work each week and whether you receive overtime pay or compensatory time off for working extra time. Find out the salary range for the position you are offered. How much can you expect to earn with annual raises? In general, hospital nurses will be paid for a determined number of hours and then asked often to work overtime for 150 percent of their hourly pay. Nurses' hourly pay may vary according to the shift they work and according to union rules, if the hospital is unionized. Typically, the evening and night shifts pay a differential above the day shift. Some hospitals have special shifts for nurses, such as 12-hour shifts three times a week that will serve as the equivalent of a full-time position. Nurses in the local professional organization may be valuable resources to explain the current local environment and particulars about specific institutions.

Visit Vault at **www.vault.com** for insider company profiles, expert advice, career message boards, expert resume reviews, the Vault Job Board and more.

VAULT CAREER LIBRARY   55

ON THE JOB

Career Paths and Lifestyles

CHAPTER 7

Nursing is a challenging profession, yet there are many opportunities to advance. Within a given institution, RNs may move from a staff to a management position, often within only a year or two. RNs may specialize and further their careers by taking additional certification or a graduate degree. RNs with flexible schedules may work part time when raising a family, then go to full time. It is very common for RNs to maintain two or more jobs at once, due to the high demand for experienced nurses and the prevalence of part-time flexible work. The career opportunities vary widely with educational preparation and work location.

Nurse with a Bachelor's Degree

Bedside nurse

Nearly every RN begins with a staff nurse position. A general medical-surgical unit is recommended for all around nursing experience. It will provide grounding in common illness, medications and treatments. After a year or two in medical-surgical, RNs typically move to another specialty unit, to home care or to intensive care. See the "A Day in the Life of a Nurse" chapter for descriptions of a typical day for a general medical-surgical staff nurse and a psychiatric inpatient staff nurse.

Occasionally, an experienced RN may move to a managerial position, especially in smaller hospitals. However, more and more, advancement into the administrative ranks is reserved for RNs with a master's degree and clinical specialization. Bedside nurse salaries rise with years of experience and level of responsibility. Generally speaking, hospital wages are higher than those in nursing homes, reflecting the more strenuous work. Bedside staff nurses may work night shifts or overtime to increase their income.

Home care nurse

The demand for home care nurses is growing. Because of the independence of the role, most agencies hire only RNs with at least a year of hospital experience. Home care nurses also may advance to manager's positions or to data management and quality assurance for the agency. Because of Medicare reporting requirements, much nursing documentation in home care is computerized and lends itself to aggregate analysis. Home care nurse salaries are generally similar to bedside nurses, although shifts are usually limited to daytime.

Public health nurse

The demand for public health and community-based nurses is also growing with the recognition that much health care relies on prevention of disease and management of chronic problems. Usually, a year or two of general medical-surgical hospital experience is needed before gaining a more independent role in community health. RNs are important for disaster preparedness and response, as well as health education in varied settings. Because nursing education pulls public health and individual health concepts together, nurses are extremely well prepared for community-based roles. See the "A Day in the Life of a Nurse" chapter for a description of the typical work of a public health nurse.

Public health nurses very commonly move up to managerial positions and have served as directors of statewide and countywide public health departments. In a managerial role, the nurse will be responsible for budget, hiring, training, staffing and quality improvement. Public health nurses may earn salaries similar to hospital bedside nurses. The working hours are usually limited to daytime, Monday to Friday.

Nurse with a Master's Degree

Nurse manager

In most large health systems, nurse managers must have a master's degree. The degree can be in administration or in a related clinical specialty. Over the course of a career, nurse managers may move up to become chief nursing officers (CNO) or chief executive officers of health systems. As gender barriers decrease, this is predicted to become more and more common. As CNO, a nurse will be responsible for the overall nursing care budget, hiring, training, staffing and quality improvement. The CNO negotiates with the governing board of the institution, the physician staff and the ancillary staff to support quality patient care by the nurses within the institution. Nurse managers make significantly more money than bedside nurses, reflecting their increased responsibilities.

Nurse practitioner

To become nationally certified, NPs need a master's degree. This allows them to practice independently, or with a physician's practice, or in an institution such as a hospital outpatient clinic or an employee health department. NPs often enjoy direct patient care so much that they do not strive to advance to managerial or other positions. However, with the changing educational milieu, the movement toward a clinical doctorate for nursing, NPs may seek further education. This will position many for roles in education, quality assurance and management. NPs do not always make more money than bedside nurses but they enjoy the independence of the role and the usual daytime schedule. Please see the "A Day in the Life of a Nurse" chapter for a typical NP day and a typical day for a nurse educator and quality assurance specialist.

Research nurse

Research nurses are commonly experienced RNs with a master's degree where they have learned the research process. Often they will mostly handle paperwork, administering research studies in a clinical institution, hospital or university for which a doctorally-prepared investigator has obtained funding. Research nurses obtain valuable experience as a stepping stone for career advancement where a doctorate is needed. Research nurses salaries are similar to bedside nurses. In order to advance, a research nurse will need further education, such as a PhD.

Nurse with a Doctoral Degree

Doctor of Philosophy

Nurses with a PhD will most likely teach and/or do research in a university. Faculty positions have rank, beginning with assistant professor, and the income is generally quite modest until reaching the full professor level. In fact, many assistant professors earn less money than their graduates, especially if they are teaching master's students. To advance in a career and in rank, a PhD-prepared nurse must publish papers and complete research

Visit Vault at **www.vault.com** for insider company profiles, expert advice,
career message boards, expert resume reviews, the Vault Job Board and more.

V/\ULT CAREER LIBRARY   **61**

studies. The most successful PhDs develop a program of research by writing grant proposals to obtain funding from the National Institutes of Health or from private foundations. More and more, top hospital nursing administrators are PhD-prepared to enhance the clinical nursing reseach and evidence-based nursing practice within their institution.

Doctor of Nursing Science

Nurses with a DNS are considered equivalent to those with a PhD.

Doctor of Nursing Practice

Nurses with a DNP are expected to be clinical experts working independently and in institutions such as hospitals and outpatient centers. They may also teach in schools of nursing. The salaries for DNP are evolving but, given the reimbursement for expert clinical care, are expected to surpass those for NPs and possibly PhDs.

Nurse with Dual Degrees

Nurse attorney

A nurse attorney is an example of a nurse with additional preparation that enhances career options and income. Nurse attorneys most likely practice independently and represent health care-related legal cases, such as malpractice. Nurse attorneys may also represent corporate clients in the health care arena. Their income is related to hours billed and is similar to that of other attorneys.

Nurse psychotherapist

A nurse psychotherapist is most likely master's prepared. In the future, nurse psychotherapists, like clinical psychologists, will be DNPs. Many psychotherapists are in private practice and bill directly for their services so their income is related to the number of patients seen and hours billed.

International Nursing

There is a wide variety of differences in education and employment in nursing throughout the world. The United States and Great Britain are seen as the standard because of the history of nursing and because of the advancement in general of Western medicine. Many other countries have advanced as well, with strong educational programs and growing respect for the profession. However, some lag behind in terms of education and also legal standing for the profession. The International Council of Nurses, working with the World Health Organization, is the major resource to bring nurses together to set standards, while recognizing the unique needs of different societies and cultures. Given that most nurses are women and, in many countries, women still do not have full citizenship and economic privileges, professional advancement in nursing is slow.

A global nursing shortage has been identified, and many nations are working to rectify it. Nurses are the "front line" staff for most health systems. In truth, many underdeveloped countries do not have an infrastructure to fully utilize highly educated and specialized physicians; they will benefit most from nurses and public health workers. Africa and Southeast Asia are the regions with the lowest nurse to population ratios. The issues most related to the worldwide nursing shortage are: 1) the impact of HIV/AIDS, 2) the migration of nurses internally and internationally, and 3) the achievement of reform and reorganization in health sectors. Opportunities for American nurses appear to be mainly in the educational and policy levels. Some schools of nursing in the U.S. have developed partnerships with schools in other countries. Asian countries, in particular, have reached out to encourage partnerships. Policy recommendations have come from the International Council of Nurses. See its web site for more specifics: www.icn.ch/global.

Changing Careers

Nurses are highly educated and skilled communicators and "people persons" who excel in many alternate careers such as management, law, politics, teaching, research and marketing. Some nurses become entrepreneurs, running their own practice or a related business. In the normal course of work, most nurses meet many, many people from all walks of life and these contacts can be very important. Many times, a natural progression will occur based on the nurse's work, the surroundings or on personal contacts over the course of the nurse's work. Other times, the nurse will make a directed effort

Visit Vault at **www.vault.com** for insider company profiles, expert advice, career message boards, expert resume reviews, the Vault Job Board and more.

VAULT CAREER LIBRARY   63

toward education in another field, such as the nurse attorneys described above. Nurses have been successful in such diverse fields as alternative health care, real estate, political office and managing national organizations such as the Red Cross and Planned Parenthood. Both within and outside of the field of nursing, there are a multitude of career choices.

Some people become interested in nursing after they've begun a career in another field. Given a previous bachelor's degree, the accelerated BSN program is perfect to gain the education required for professional nursing practice. Many universities offer a combined accelerated BSN/MSN so that one could, within about three years, gain both degrees and be prepared for advanced nursing practice as a nurse administrator or nurse practitioner. It is expected, as advanced practice evolves to the doctoral level, that combined BSN/DNP educational programs will become more prevalent. Second career nurses often bring their previous skills into their nursing careers. For example, an elementary teacher turned pediatric nurse practitioner will be very familiar with growth and development and family issues that pertain to her or his new role in health care. A computer programmer turned nurse informaticist can be quite skilled in translating the data needs of health care into "computerese."

Nursing Uppers and Downers

CHAPTER 8

People who choose to become nurses often do it because they want to make a difference in the lives of others. They like a personal connection with other people and to see the effects they have on health and well-being. In contrast to teaching, where the effects of one's work are sometimes slowly building up over years, nursing is very dynamic and can show effects very quickly. The following are some of the benefits, risks and challenges of pursuing a career in nursing.

Benefits

Nurses are satisfied to successfully help other people with their problems. Nurses have the opportunity to change another's life for the better. Nurses work with people, as opposed to working with papers, machines or merchandise. The breadth of the field allows for job changes over time. Many positions are available with part-time and flexible schedules to accommodate family responsibilities. Nursing knowledge is valuable for one's personal and family health.

Risks

Education below the bachelor's level is offered for nurses, yet a person with lower level education will have a limited career path and limited income. A separate license is needed for each state. The license application process can be very lengthy and take up to several months. Some states require fingerprints and a criminal background investigation.

Compensation for nurses varies tremendously. Beginning compensation is relatively good but there seems to be a "ceiling" in compensation for advanced careers. Nursing is a traditionally female occupation and vestiges of a male doctor-female nurse power structure remain, though this is changing.

Due to the variety of education and positions for nurses, each nurse may need to clearly describe his/her education and skills. And hospital nursing, in particular, is very demanding with a risk of physical and emotional overload.

According to one researcher, the nursing profession as a whole has made several costly mistakes. The first mistake nurses made was to sell their services to hospitals and other institutions, rather than directly to patients, as doctors do. Because of this, nurses lost control of their working conditions. In addition, they tend to work under doctors' orders, so their autonomy is sometimes compromised. They also allied themselves with orthodox medicine, which tends to promote symptom suppression through pharmaceuticals, as opposed to other kinds of interventions. Because of these decisions, nursing may have remained more static and less dynamic than other medical professions.

Challenges

Professional nurses face challenges in many arenas related to their historical position in the health care team. The position of a professional is one of authority within a defined body of knowledge. In contrast to self-employed professionals such as physicians and others, over the years, nurses have commonly worked as employees of hospitals, physicians, health departments or other agencies. Furthermore, the body of knowledge unique to nursing has only recently begun to be defined through research. Handicapped by its history of being a woman's vocation, nursing is just now coming into its own as an independent and respected profession.

A large challenge related to nursing's history is the low income ceiling for nurses. While many people are attracted to the profession by the relatively high starting income, financial pressures within the health care industry, as well as the continued predominant position of nurses as employees, limits nurses' salary range. It is hoped that increasing the data on patient outcomes and high quality care that are related to nursing interventions will turn the tide on this issue. In addition, the rise of the doctor of nursing practice may benefit nurses' incomes.

An additional challenge is the lack of public financial support for nursing education. Nursing educators commonly have lower incomes than their graduates! Consequently, there is a shortage of qualified nursing faculty. Many times the demands of teaching, academic service and research preclude nurse faculty practice and the additional income it brings to professional schools such as medicine and dentistry. In contrast to expensive medical education, about half of which is funded by tax dollars, public financing for much less expensive registered nurse and nurse practitioner education is quite limited. Yet, currently we have a surplus of physicians and a shortage of nurses in the U.S. A comprehensive evaluation of either nursing or medical education has not taken place since the Flexner report (for medical education) and the Goldmark report (for nursing education) in the early 1900s. Due to strong legislative lobby efforts by the American Medical Association (AMA), this imbalance in public funding is not likely to change in the near future without a large public outcry.

Job hazards

Most RNs work in comfortable institutional settings. Some nurses travel to patients' homes, schools, community centers and other sites. Many RN positions entail considerable walking, standing and other physical exertion. According to the Occupational Safety and Health Administration, the primary hazard in patient care is blood borne pathogens, such as hepatitis B and HIV. Nurses are also exposed to a variety of other infectious diseases. RNs must observe standards and guidelines to protect themselves against disease and related dangers in the health care environment, such as risks from radiation, accidental needle sticks, contaminated splashes, chemicals used for sterilization and medications. RNs are vulnerable to back injury from lifting and moving patients, electrical shocks from a variety of equipment, and fire and inhalation hazards from compressed gases such as oxygen and anesthesia.

RNs are subject to emotional strain from work with suffering patients and families as well as from strenuous job demands. For example, RNs may work with severely injured, mentally ill and permanently debilitated patients and consequently, will see families come to grips with bad news. RNs may work with dying patients of all ages. In addition, even when they may be working overtime and caring for a number of other patients, RNs are responsible for accurate assessments and treatments and for timely communication of key information to physicians and other responsible providers.

Turnover

National RN turnover is high; it is estimated at 15 percent. The physical demands of the work, including patient lifting, walking long corridors and standing, high patient care loads and long, rotating shift work schedules may cause older, experienced nurses to leave the workforce. In the past, the frequency of lack of recognition and advancement over a career and the often slow increase in fair compensation for valuable years of experience (as described above in the challenges section) has discouraged nurses from

Visit Vault at **www.vault.com** for insider company profiles, expert advice, career message boards, expert resume reviews, the Vault Job Board and more.

VAULT CAREER LIBRARY   **67**

hospital work. However, this opens opportunities for new graduates and RNs who are willing to take on hospital shifts outside the usual Monday through Friday, 9-to-5 pattern. These positions may be particularly available in high turnover areas, such as critical care units, emergency departments and operating rooms. Also, RNs have myriad work opportunities beyond the hospital. Jobs beyond the hospital include home care, public health, teaching, research and the like.

A national survey of RNs done by the Bureau of Health Professions found that, of currently employed nurses, about 78 percent were satisfied (about 27 percent were estimated to be extremely satisfied with their principal nursing position and 50.5 percent moderately satisfied). Only13.8 percent of nurses employed in nursing were dissatisfied. Research has shown that nurses are more satisfied when they have a voice in hospital governance. About 14 percent of RNs were not working in nursing in 2004; 42.7 percent left for unspecified reasons connected with the workplace.

First-Person Accounts

The following quotes are from nurses who wrote with pride in Internet blogs of the benefits they feel in their work.

- *"I am proud to call myself a nurse because I can't think of any other profession that has so much to offer. I graduated in 1971 from the University of Washington. Then in 1993, I went back for my master's and graduated in 1998 with a master's in nursing leadership. In my 34 years of nursing, I have worked in a variety of areas. Currently I am working as a cardiac rehabilitation nurse. I started on a woman's surgical floor, and I have also worked in the operating room, recovery room, emergency room, labor and delivery, post partum, critical care and home health nursing.*

- *"My variable experiences have shown me the many opportunities nursing can provide. Nursing can take you wherever you want or wherever you dream, 'the sky is the limit.' That is why I am proud to tell everyone that I am a nurse."*

- *"The thing that amazes me the most is not how much has changed in the nursing/medical arena, but that I have not changed. That is, even though I have been involved in so many different areas of nursing and the nursing field itself is almost unrecognizable from my beginning time, I find that I stay in it for the very same reasons I became a nurse in the first place. Those are, very simply put, love for the human race and my patients. To be a part of the process that takes the pain from their eyes, to see the peace settle across their face, to hear the sigh of relief, to gently touch their fears away, and then, quietly move away, knowing I made a difference in someone's life today is why I chose nursing and why I stay in it, even today at 62 years of age."*

- *"Thirty years ago, when I entered the workforce as a new graduate, I would not have guessed the many ways that nursing would allow me to make a difference. From burn critical care to public health, to rehabilitation, and now in research, at every turn, a common theme emerged: here were opportunities to express the deepest closeness to humanity, and to use the work of my heart and my hands toward making life better. I always considered it a privilege and a sacred trust to be a part of people's important moments—whether in pain or fear, whether facing the challenge of a life-changing event, whether learning to care for themselves—my words and actions take on heightened importance. I was there in these patient's important moments, and whatever I said or did would stay with them from that point forward.*

- *"It is this durable sense of meaningfulness that kept me going through the years of grueling shift work, the heavy burdens, the short-staffing, the expected and unexpected. Being a nurse is not just a job, it is a feature of who I am. The best that is in me is expressed in the work of nursing."*

Other Factors

Like any industry, external factors will affect one's career. Below, we discuss the external factors that affect careers in nursing, including policy issues, salaries and benefits, and diversity in the workplace.

Policy issues

Policy issues in nursing pertain to the profession and to health care in general. Women are still a much unappreciated resource in many countries. As long as the majority of nurses are women, subtle gender discrimination will influence the advancement of the profession. Perhaps things will change

Visit Vault at **www.vault.com** for insider company profiles, expert advice, career message boards, expert resume reviews, the Vault Job Board and more.

VAULT CAREER LIBRARY   **69**

when the number of women in the U.S. Congress or Supreme Court is equal to that of men.

Policy usually boils down to the allocation of resources and money. The nursing profession is vested in "equal pay for equal work," showing the areas of overlap between nursing and other professions. This agenda has been successful in the equal reimbursement of NPs and physicians by federal payers and many others. However, barriers remain in managed care plan restrictions to NPs. Another policy issue for nursing is prescriptive authority. At the present time, NPs may prescribe medications in all 50 states; however, there remain a variety of restrictions and permissions around prescriptive authority that nurses wish to change.

The American Nurses Association (ANA) is the premier voice for nursing in federal policy issues. Each state has an organization that participates in the ANA federation. All nurses are encouraged to join ANA to support the lobbying and policy work that it does (see www.ana.org). A variety of other nursing organizations are active in policy issues, including the American Academy of NPs, the National Nursing Centers Consortium and others.

Salaries and benefits

The median annual salary of registered nurses in the U.S. was $52,330 in May 2004, according to the US. Department of Labor. The middle 50 percent earned between $43,370 and $63,360.

Annual earnings ranged from less than $37,300 to more than $74,760. The following table shows median annual earnings in several settings where the largest numbers of registered nurses worked in May 2004:

Employment services:	$63,170
General medical and surgical hospitals:	$53,450
Home health care services:	$48,990
Offices of physicians:	$48,250
Nursing care facilities:	$48,220

from bhpr.hrsa.gov/healthworkforce/reports/nursing/samplesurvey04preliminary/default.htm

Salaries reflect position as well as education level. For example, a nurse manager will usually make at least 10 percent more than staff nurses in the same institution. Most nurse managers have a master's degree, whereas a staff nurse tends to have only a bachelor's degree. A nurse manager may make upwards of $150,000 per year.

The average annual NP income, another position requiring a master's degree, was about $75,000 across the U.S. in 2005. But the salaries of research nurses, who also have master's degrees, are more similar to bedside nurses, with the average being about $53,000 per year.

Salaries of doctors of nursing practice will most likely be in the range of $100,000 per year.

Most nursing positions offer standard benefits like health and life insurance, and many employers offer flexible work schedules, child care, educational benefits and bonuses. About one in four RNs works part time.

Nursing provides unique opportunities for all ages, genders, ethnicities and languages. In 2004, about 27 percent of registered nurses in the U.S. were under the age of 40. The largest group is between ages 40 and 54. Nursing has traditionally been regarded as a women's profession; in 2004, 5.7 percent of registered nurses were male, but that is changing as salaries rise. There is still a gap between the growing ethnic diversity in the U.S. overall and that within nursing. It is likely that weaknesses in public education at the elementary and secondary levels have contributed to this gap (IOM). In 2004, 88.4 percent of RNs were white, non-Hispanic, according to the U.S. Department of Health and Human Services. Because of the especially rapid increase in the immigrant population, nurses who speak English plus a second language are in tremendous demand.

Diversity in the workforce

Major demographic changes are occurring in the United States, including a rapid increase in the percentages of residents who are nonwhite, who speak primary languages other than English, and who have diverse values and beliefs regarding health and health care. Efforts to mirror the overall population diversity in nursing and other health professions, however, have been hampered by gross inequalities in the quality of primary and secondary education for students of different racial and ethnic groups. Given the Institute of Medicine's research that shows a positive association between "greater diversity among health professionals, improved access to care for racial and ethnic minority patients, greater patient choice and satisfaction,

Visit Vault at **www.vault.com** for insider company profiles, expert advice, career message boards, expert resume reviews, the Vault Job Board and more.

VAULT CAREER LIBRARY

71

better patient-provider communication, and better educational experiences for all students while in training," promoting diversity in nursing is a high priority.

A Day in the Life of a Nurse

CHAPTER 9

Medical-Surgical Hospital Nurse

Dan Bratton, RN, BSN, works rotating shifts at the medium-sized (220 beds) Good Samaritan General Hospital. For two weeks, Dan works 7 a.m. to 3:30 p.m., the next two weeks will be 3 to 11:30 p.m., and the next two weeks will be 11 p.m. to 7:30 a.m. (The 30 minutes overlap between shifts gives the nurses that are leaving some time to report to the nurses taking over the important events that pertain to each patient.) Dan graduated six months ago and this is his first position in a medical-surgical unit. Today, Dan is working the day shift, 7 a.m. to 3:30 p.m. The day shift is busy because this is when physicians come in to see their patients and many diagnostic tests and therapies are scheduled.

6:45 a.m. Dan arrives a few minutes early so he can change into his hospital-supplied scrub suit and get himself organized for the day.

7:00 a.m. Dan's supervisor gives him a list of eight patients to care for. Dan knows two of the patients from his previous shift; six of the patients are new. They range in age from 25 to 85 and their diagnoses include diabetes mellitus, congestive heart failure, two days post-stroke and acute renal failure.

7:05 a.m. Dan listens to the report of all the nurses going off shift, paying particular attention to his eight patients. Because the report is tape recorded, any questions must be asked of the night shift leader.

7:30 a.m. Dan goes to the patients' records to check each care plan, describing tasks and schedules for the day. Each patient's physician will be coming in early to go around to see his/her patients. Dan will check on any discharges scheduled and any therapy or diagnostic testing that requires the patient to travel to another area of the hospital. Then he plans his day around these events and the medication and care schedule for each patient.

8:00 a.m. Dan accompanies the physicians to report on any changes in the past 24 hours and to gather information on what is next in the physician's plan. He discovers that the diabetic patient is to be discharged to go home and he will meet with family members to reinforce the self-care needed to balance treatment for diabetes: exercise, nutrition and medication. Also, one of the post-stroke patients is going to be moved to a rehabilitation facility.

Dan talks with those family members to answer questions, provide reassurance and explain the goals of rehab. He shows them an Internet site, www.medlineplus.gov, where they can find specific information about stroke, appropriate rehabilitation, safety and home care, and any medications that may be prescribed later.

9:00 a.m. Dan receives and stores the single-dose medications for his patients that have been brought to the unit by a pharmacy technician. He has to check the physicians' documentation for new orders, and authorize them and set them in motion for each of his eight patients. The day goes very quickly, even without any real crises arising. Medications and treatments must be given before patients go to their therapy with rehabilitation or before they go to have radiology testing or treatments.

10:00 a.m. Most of the patient discharges occur before noon. The patients who are going home need to have specific discharge instructions as well as an escort to leave the hospital safely. As soon as one patient leaves, another is admitted, so Dan greets the new patient and completes paperwork setting up a nursing care plan.

11:00 a.m. Dan "rounds" on his patients again before lunch to check blood pressures and other vital signs and to keep an eye on everyone.

12:00 noon This is a good day. Dan gets to relax and eat lunch with a colleague. They discuss a continuing education program on diabetes that they will attend over the weekend. According to their state board of nursing regulations, they need 30 hours of continuing education every two years in order to renew their license to practice.

12:30 p.m. Dan and his colleague return to work. He sees that one of his patients has called for help. When he goes to the patient's room, he finds that she became dizzy and has fallen on her way to the toilet. He helps her back to bed and assesses her condition. Fortunately, she appears to have no broken bones and the dizziness has passed. He cautions the patient not to stand up quickly but to give herself a couple of minutes sitting at the bedside before standing and walking. He also encourages her to seek assistance when she wants to get out of bed. After checking the patient's medication list, Dan phones the patient's physician and suggests some medication changes that may decrease the patient's tendency toward dizziness. Dan knows that the circumstances around this event are very important because his hospital is working to decrease the overall rate of falls and patient injuries.

1:30 p.m. By this time, Dan must administer another round of medications and treatments to his patient group. He checks the physician orders to find new IVs, blood tests and referrals were ordered. Dan checks with the unit secretary to see that these were ordered. Dan talks with one of the medical school students about patient falls and how to prevent them.

2:30 p.m. Dan speaks with a nursing school faculty member on the telephone. She is looking for a clinical practice site for students in the summer rotation. He agrees to work with undergraduate student nurses and to recruit fellow staff nurses to take other nurses. He does a final round to check each patient's condition before he leaves for the day.

3:00 p.m. Dan gives a report to the group of nurses coming on for the next shift. He speaks to his supervisor regarding his preference for next month's schedule that is being planned. (Some hospitals have made self-scheduling available to the nursing staff.) Then, Dan has a few moments to document the care he provided during the past eight hours. He enters data into a computerized record that contains easy templates for routine care. After that, it is time to relax for a moment!

Psychiatric Hospital Nurse

Mary Johnson, RN, BSN, is a psychiatric nurse working on a medical psychiatric unit in a large, 600-bed hospital. Mary has worked on this unit for the past four years. Prior to this, she worked in home care and also as a medical-surgical nurse. She has seen many psych issues in patients in all settings. Most commonly, patients come from the emergency room to stay for 10 days when they are deemed a danger to themselves or others. From here, they will either be discharged for outpatient therapy, or, if their illness is quite serious, they will go to a specialty psychiatric hospital in a city about 50 miles away. Every day, Mary sees people in great distress and agitation. She has learned to be very patient and to listen to people who may not make logical statements. Today, Mary is working the evening shift, 3 to 11:30 p.m.

2:45 p.m. Mary arrives a few minutes early so she can hang up her coat and get ready for the evening. She speaks to a couple of nurses from the day shift about local master's education programs; the three of them are planning to apply to a psychiatric nurse practitioner program. Mary wears regular street clothes to help decrease the anxiety of the patients.

3:00 p.m. Mary speaks to her head nurse to discover her assignment for this evening. She has eight patients, all of whom she cared for yesterday. Mary's patients range in age from 27 to 66. Their diagnoses include chronic schizophrenia, bipolar disorder and major depression. Two of them have

Visit Vault at **www.vault.com** for insider company profiles, expert advice, career message boards, expert resume reviews, the Vault Job Board and more.

VAULT CAREER LIBRARY   **75**

been admitted previously and Mary knows them. The other six are new. Most of the psych patients stay for about two to three weeks, until they stabilize on medication. Occasionally, a patient will be admitted under a court order, that is, they were deemed a danger to themselves or others, and they may choose to leave after the 10-day holding period expires.

3:05 p.m. Mary participates in the shift report, learning key events of the day from the nurses who will leave at 3:30. The shift report on her unit is live, not recorded, so nurses can discuss the best management of these challenging psych patients on a daily basis.

3:30 p.m. Mary looks over the patient records from the last two shifts, since she was here before. She checks to see that the meds for each of her patients are stored on the unit. She sketches out a schedule for herself for the evening.

4:00 p.m. Mary "rounds" to say hello to each of her patients, take their blood pressure and see what their immediate needs are. She adds specific plans to her personal schedule for the evening.

4:30 p.m. Mary distributes the scheduled 5 p.m. medications to her patients. She records the meds and times they were given. She notices that one patient is missing a medication that will be due at 10 p.m., so she phones the pharmacy to investigate why the proper med is not on the unit and to arrange for a special delivery.

5:30 p.m. Mary talks with one of her patients who will be discharged tomorrow. He is worried about going home and switching to an outpatient therapist. She encourages him to write down some of his fears and, together, they discuss what he can do.

6:00 p.m. Mary has one patient who was admitted yesterday and who is very withdrawn. She goes to this patient's room and, in a friendly way, brings her out to the dining room to join the others for dinner. Because the psych patients are ambulatory, they are expected to participate in group meals and activities. Mary eats dinner with one or another of her patients every evening.

7:00 p.m. This is the visiting period. Family members often come to speak with their loved one in the hospital and many of them want a few minutes with Mary to ask about their loved one's condition and what is next. Often, Mary talks with patients' families to explain their symptoms and the available treatments. She will also provide hope to patients and their families about the timeline and effectiveness of treatments. When she hears terrible stories, she listens and then tries to let the stories go through her, so that she does not keep horrible histories in her own mind and heart. She wants to be able to listen to the grief and sorrow of people who have lost someone dear to them. She will talk with them to encourage them to pick up the pieces of their lives and move ahead.

8:30 p.m. Now there is exercise time, and everyone goes to the gym. Research has found that exercise decreases depression. Also, evening exercise promotes sleep at a later hour; sometimes the psych patients are sleepy due to the side effects of their medications yet, if they go to sleep too early, they will not sleep well through the night. Some of the patients participate in an impromptu volleyball game. Others watch the game or go to the treadmill and weight room to work out. Recreational staff coordinate the gym time and the nurses participate as they wish.

10:00 p.m. Everyone returns to the psych unit and begins to prepare for bedtime. Mary administers the 10 p.m. medications and spends a few minutes with each of her eight patients. She listens to a couple of people who have injected dangerous drugs into themselves and developed the non-curable disease HIV. She teaches these people how to protect themselves and their partners from the contagious illness.

11:00 p.m. Mary participates in the evening report to the night staff. Most of the patients will sleep at night but a few insomniacs and those adjusting to new medications may be up, roaming the halls. It will be left to the day staff to get them out of bed to reschedule their sleep-wake cycle.

Mary is very skilled at mental status assessment and can start to figure out the etiology of a change in mental status, whether it be alcohol/drug withdrawal, overdose, stroke or other organic problem. She cares for adolescents with eating disorders who have run away from home, drug addicts who have lost their jobs, psychotics and schizophrenics who hear voices in their heads, and elderly Alzheimer's patients who cannot remember their children's names. She has to know how to care for many common acute and chronic illnesses that her psychiatric patients have along with their mental health problems.

Mary cares for homeless people, the middle class, and the rich and famous. She says, "Psychiatry is about having broad nursing skills, being autonomous and a patient advocate. Most of all, you have to be willing to use your hands, eyes, ears, nursing instinct and your heart to do your job."

Family Nurse Practitioner

Carina Sanchez is a family nurse practitioner with 10 years' experience. She works at a migrant health center in rural North Carolina. The center receives

Visit Vault at **www.vault.com** for insider company profiles, expert advice, career message boards, expert resume reviews, the Vault Job Board and more.

VAULT CAREER LIBRARY

77

grant funding from the federal government so that it can provide primary health care to uninsured families. Most of the patients are Spanish-speaking, so her bilingual skills are a huge asset to the practice. As a family NP, Carina sees people of all ages.

8:45 a.m. Carina arrives and checks her schedule for the day. She has 10 patients scheduled for the morning session that runs from 9 a.m. to 1 p.m. Another 10 are scheduled for the afternoon, 2 to 5 p.m. About half of the patients keep their appointments. But, she will probably be busy because the center accepts walk-in patients who come without an appointment for an urgent problem. Carina has a student FNP working with her. The student sees every patient first, then presents the case to Carina who goes back with the student to complete the encounter. Carina is not paid for precepting the student, but she does get a clinical faculty appointment with the school of nursing and a discount on the continuing education courses they offer. She feels a professional obligation to contribute to nursing education in any way that she can.

9:00 a.m. The first patient is a two-month old baby boy, Miguel, here for a routine checkup. He is weighed by the nursing assistant and Carina speaks to the mother about how he is feeding. She finds that he is breastfeeding and that the mother did not know she could receive WIC foods for herself while breastfeeding. (WIC is a federal program, funded through the Department of Agriculture, that provides food coupons for pregnant and nursing mothers and infants up to age 5.) There is a WIC program next door to the health center so the mother is directed to go there after the checkup. Carina examines Miguel and orders routine vaccinations for him. She talks to the mother about safety and child development and family planning. Miguel will return in two months. His mother needs a family planning visit later in the week.

9:30 a.m. Next is a 50-year-old overweight man who has back pain. Carina looks over his lab records to find that his blood sugar and blood cholesterol have been rising over the past couple of years. She speaks to him about the relationship between his weight and all of his problems. After giving him instructions for over-the-counter pain medications and back stretching exercises, she refers him to see the dietician down the hall.

10:00 a.m. The next patient is a teenage girl, presenting with a vaginal discharge. Her mother has brought her to the health center but she graciously goes to the waiting room when Carina reminds her that the visit is confidential. Without her mother's presence, the teen admits to sexual activity so Carina does a pregnancy test and an exam checking for infection with a sexually transmitted disease. By looking at the discharge under the microscope, Carina diagnoses a simple yeast infection, treatable with over-the-counter medication. She prescribes the morning after pill and counsels the teen on safe sex and more effective birth control.

11:00 a.m. The next three patients are here for routine follow up of high blood pressure. Carina checks their diets and medications and makes sure that they have routine lab work every 6 months. Two of them are overweight but only 1 agrees to see the dietician this time.

12:00 noon Lunch time. Carina takes the time to check her telephone and e-mail messages and respond. She has time to review a couple of journals to keep up with new developments in health care. She eats lunch with the dietician and they begin to plan a group education series for diabetics who need to learn how to balance diet, exercise and medications to control their blood sugars. The FNP student will be involved with this also as part of her community project.

1:00 p.m. Next is a well woman checkup for a 45-year-old. The patient wants to discuss symptoms of menopause. She also needs an exam with screening for cervical and colon cancer. Carina watches the student complete the exam and arranges a referral for mammogram. She counsels the patient on diet and exercise to stay healthy as she ages.

1:45 p.m. Next are a couple of walk-in patients with cough and fever. Neither one is terribly ill but they are miserable and would like some medication. Because their illness is probably viral, no antibiotics will help and the best medication is over-the-counter. One of the patients is found to have large cavities in the lower right molars so is referred to the dental clinic also run by the health center.

2:30 p.m. Another child comes in, a 12-year-old, here for a school physical. Carina has a supply of the forms needed to show that required examinations were done. She checks the immunization record to find that this child needs a booster of tetanus, diphtheria and pertussis vaccines. Also she counsels the preteen on drugs, sex, and rock 'n' roll to hopefully prevent future problems.

3:00 p.m. An elderly woman comes in next. She has borderline diabetes, controlled by diet and one oral medication. She also has high blood pressure, well controlled. Her medications and her lab work are reviewed every three months. She is encouraged to keep up her daily walking schedule and to participate in activities she enjoys, such as her painting class.

Visit Vault at **www.vault.com** for insider company profiles, expert advice, career message boards, expert resume reviews, the Vault Job Board and more.

V/\ULT CAREER LIBRARY   **79**

3:30 p.m. A young man comes in to have his stitches removed. He had gone to the emergency room a week ago after lacerating his knee. The wound healed well without any infection and the stitches come out easily.

4:15 p.m. Carina checks her messages again to return calls and e-mails before the end of the day. She reviews the patient list for the next day and asks the nursing assistant to check that lab reports are available for those patients. Carina is "on call" tonight, so she checks with the other providers, two physicians and a pediatric NP, to see if they expect anyone to call.

5:00 p.m. This is a good day, Carina leaves on time! However, she may need another hour or so to answer questions and arrange care for anyone who calls in during the night.

Public Health Nurse

Tanisha Jackson is a public health nurse. She works in the TB (tuberculosis) control clinic in a large city health department. The clinic oversees the treatment of community-residing patients who receive daily medications for TB. It also does TB screening and follow up for city residents. From time to time, it will sponsor health information events to raise awareness of TB prevalence, free screening and treatment. Because the HIV infection rate in the city is quite high, TB control has risen as a public health issue. Tanisha works 9 to 5, Monday through Friday, in a government position with full benefits.

9:00 a.m. Tanisha begins the daily open hours for directly observed TB treatment. The patients who attend this morning clinic are high risk for developing drug-resistant TB. Therefore, their treatment must be observed to see that the medication is taken each and every day. Tanisha greets each one and keeps careful records with updated contact information. She also coordinates with other treatments these patients may get, such as methadone maintenance and HIV services.

11:00 a.m. Now the TB screening service is open. People who have family contacts to TB or who need screening for their job will walk in to have a ppd skin test done. Then, 48 to 72 hours later, they return to have it checked and documentation completed that the screening was negative. If they have had a positive skin test, Tanisha arranges for them to have a chest x-ray for step two in the screening process. A radiologist reads the x-ray and the NP working in the TB clinic will order sputum testing to confirm TB if the x-ray seems to indicate it. Otherwise, the NP will order the preventive INH medication. Usually these patients take the medication on their own. They will not be added to the group that Tanisha observes daily.

1:00 p.m. Lunch is over and Tanisha meets with the nursing director to coordinate educational outreach to the area's homeless shelters and food kitchens. Because of the high turnover of homeless people in the area, outreach is done on a regular basis. This afternoon, Tanisha herself will make the rounds, bringing printed material about TB and about the free services at the public clinic.

2:00 to 5:00 p.m. Tanisha walks and buses to the nearby outreach sites. At each one, she speaks to the coordinator and also answers questions posed by potential patients. She invites everyone to the clinic for the free services. Her friendly manner will encourage people to come for what may be an unknown or frightening experience. Tanisha had a neighbor who died of TB about five years ago, so she is committed to control of the disease.

Nurse Informaticist

Terry Lee is a nurse informaticist at the local health sciences center. She works with a team of people who are implementing a new patient record software, unit by unit. She is responsible for coordinating with the nursing managers for three large units. One has already begun to use the software, the other two are in varying stages of planning to "go live."

9:00 a.m. Terry organizes her day by checking messages and scheduling meetings with the nurse managers on the units she watches over.

9:30 a.m. Terry meets with the director of the implementation project. Each member of the team reports briefly on current status and immediate goals. Once a week they meet to touch base as a group. Every other week, they spend more time in a planning session to schedule the next moves.

10:00 a.m. Terry visits the unit that is actively using the system. She checks with a couple of key people about any current issues. She makes phone calls to trouble shoot with the pharmacy about documentation and the link to the supply of medications coming to the unit.

11:00 a.m. Terry visits the unit where "go live" with the software is planned for next week. She discusses the training plan with the nurse manager. They decide on a unit "champion" who will be the most enthusiastic user and will be the on-site support for the rollout.

Visit Vault at **www.vault.com** for insider company profiles, expert advice, career message boards, expert resume reviews, the Vault Job Board and more.

VAULT CAREER LIBRARY

81

12:00 noon Lunch time. After lunch, Terry checks her telephone and email messages and follows up.

1:00 p.m. Terry visits the third unit that will not "go live" until next month. She meets with the nurse manager and the unit secretary to discuss custom fitting according to the work of that unit. She demonstrates the software currently in use and discusses training issues that may arise when the time draws closer.

3:00 p.m. Terry communicates with the software representative about the previous meetings. She advocates for the custom fitting and negotiates a timetable with the software rep. Then she communicates this to her supervisor, so the plan is confirmed. The day has been spent in meetings and other communications. Terry has not touched a patient but has planned the software and workflow to facilitate safe and effective patient care by others in the hospital.

Nurse Educator

Jackie Fowler is a professor of nursing at a highly ranked university. She teaches two doctoral courses and manages a research study, in addition to writing articles and participating on school and university committees. She often works from home, managing student course work online. Today, she is in the office.

10:00 a.m. Jackie arrives and checks her e-mail. She has brought papers to return to the 12 students in her morning doctoral class. Class goes from 4:30 to 7 p.m. so that working students can be accommodated.

10:30 a.m. Jackie checks with her research manager about current issues in the study. The research study follows breastfeeding women over time to gather information on daily challenges that promote or prohibit breastfeeding. Some of the research participants work full time, some part time, and some are not back to work. The groups' responses will be contrasted and compared in the analysis.

11:30 a.m. Jackie now walks across campus for a lunch meeting with the university institutional review board. She represents the school of nursing on the IRB committee. This is an important part of the university because it oversees the protection of human subjects in all university-sponsored research projects.

2:00 p.m. Now Jackie is back in her office, catching up on telephone messages and e-mails. She is involved in recruiting doctoral students for the next class, so she speaks to some of her old friends in area hospitals and schools to market the program. She also puts the finishing touches on her PowerPoint presentation for the class that begins at 4:30. And she completes the grading of the latest assignment and records the grades.

4:30 p.m. Now class begins and the next two-and-a-half hours are full of thinking and discussion about research design. Three students present examples of specific designs from published articles and lead the discussion.

Quality Assurance Nurse Specialist

Joe Moore is a BSN who works as a quality assurance specialist in a large health insurance company. He reviews electronic documentation and analyzes the match between research-based guidelines and the documented care. His work will be fed back to the physicians and nurses who have managed care contracts with the insurer so that they will receive incentive payments for meeting goals to improve care.

9:00 a.m. Joe arrives at work and checks his messages. He prepares reports for a meeting later in the day.

10:00 a.m. Joe goes to his computer where he left off yesterday in the midst of analyzing the data related to diabetic care for a large outpatient physician practice. The practice employs NPs, family practice physicians, internal medicine physicians and endocrinologists, all of whom care for diabetic patients. While the data are useful for the individual physicians to show how they meet national guidelines, the insurer also is examining the differences between individual providers and different specialties to make decisions about contract negotiations. Therefore, Joe is looking at several variables and at data from several sources.

12:00 to 5 p.m. At lunch, Joe travels to a meeting where he will learn more about selection of variables for analysis of different patient conditions. He will get continuing education credit for his attendance, which he needs to renew his state-issued RN license next year. He is fortunate to have his employer provide time and tuition for this kind of benefit.

Visit Vault at **www.vault.com** for insider company profiles, expert advice, career message boards, expert resume reviews, the Vault Job Board and more.

VAULT CAREER LIBRARY   **83**

Use the Internet's
MOST TARGETED
job search tools.

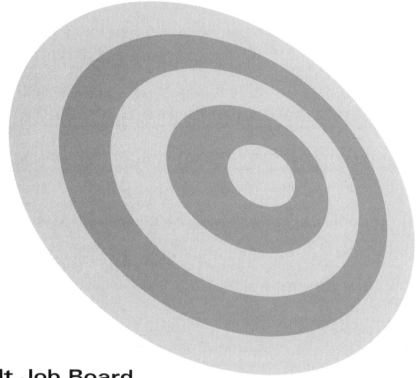

Vault Job Board

Target your search by industry, function, and experience level, and find the job openings that you want.

VaultMatch Resume Database

Vault takes match-making to the next level: post your resume and customize your search by industry, function, experience and more. We'll match job listings with your interests and criteria and e-mail them directly to your inbox.

> the most trusted name in career information™

Final Analysis

Nursing is a challenging and rewarding career and can be many careers over time. When one desires to work with people and to take responsibility to assist others, nursing is a good choice. Nurses can always find work and the starting income of an RN is relatively high. A four-year degree, a Bachelor of Science in Nursing (BSN) is highly recommended as the starting point for a lifelong career of advancement in this exciting profession.

Visit Vault at **www.vault.com** for insider company profiles, expert advice, career message boards, expert resume reviews, the Vault Job Board and more.

VAULT CAREER LIBRARY   85

APPENDIX

Organizations and Helpful Web Sites

For information on a career as a registered nurse and nursing education, contact:

- National League for Nursing, 61 Broadway, New York, NY 10006. Internet: www.nln.org

For information on nursing career options, financial aid and listings of BSN, graduate and accelerated nursing programs, contact:

- American Association of Colleges of Nursing, 1 Dupont Circle NW, Suite 530, Washington, DC 20036. Internet: www.aacn.nche.edu

For additional information on registered nurses, including credentialing, contact:

- American Nurses Association, 8515 Georgia Ave., Suite 400, Silver Spring, MD 20910. Internet: nursingworld.org

For information on the NCLEX-RN exam and a list of individual states' boards of nursing, contact:

- National Council of State Boards of Nursing, 111 E. Wacker Dr., Suite 2900, Chicago, IL 60611. Internet: www.ncsbn.org

For information on obtaining U.S. certification and work visas for foreign-educated nurses, contact:

- Commission on Graduates of Foreign Nursing Schools, 3600 Market St., Suite 400, Philadelphia, PA 19104. Internet: www.cgfns.org

For a list of accredited clinical nurse specialist programs, contact:

- National Association of Clinical Nurse Specialists, 2090 Linglestown Rd., Suite 107, Harrisburg, PA 17110. Internet: www.nacns.org/cnsdirectory.shtml

For information on nurse anesthetists, including a list of accredited programs, contact:

- American Association of Nurse Anesthetists, 222 Prospect Ave., Park Ridge, IL 60068. Internet: www.aana.com

For information on nurse midwives, including a list of accredited programs, contact:

- American College of Nurse-Midwives, 8403 Colesville Rd., Suite 1550, Silver Spring, MD 20910. Internet: www.midwife.org

Visit Vault at **www.vault.com** for insider company profiles, expert advice, career message boards, expert resume reviews, the Vault Job Board and more.

VAULT CAREER LIBRARY

89

For information on nurse practitioners, including a list of accredited programs, contact:

- American Academy of Nurse Practitioners, P.O. Box 12846, Austin, TX 78711. Internet: www.aanp.org

Some resources cited by the U.S. Bureau of Labor Statistics are:

- *CareerOneStop:* www.CareerOneStop.org, (877) 348-0502
- *America's Job Bank:* www.ajb.org
- *America's Career InfoNet:* www.acinet.org
- *America's Service Locator:* www.servicelocator.org

Some business directories where you may find information at the library or online include:

- *Dun & Bradstreet's Million Dollar Directory*
- *Standard and Poor's Register of Corporations*
- *Mergent's Industrial Review* (formerly *Moody's Industrial Manual*)
- *Thomas Register of American Manufacturers*
- *Ward's Business Directory*

Selected nursing blogs:

- www.emergiblog.com/2006/06/change-of-shift-volume-one-number-one.html
- medscapenursing.blogs.com/?src=mp

References and Recommended Reading

Benner, P. (2001). *From Novice to Expert: Excellence and Power in Clinical Nursing Practice.* Menlo Park, California: Prentice Hall.

Benner, P., Tanner, C. A., & Chesla, C. A. (1997). "Becoming an Expert Nurse." *American Journal of Nursing*, 97(6), 1-4.

D'Antonio, Patricia (2004). "Women, Nursing, and Baccalaureate Education in 20th Century America." *Journal of Nursing Scholarship* 36 (4), 379-384.

Easter, M. (2005). *What I do.* Medscape nursing blog. medscapenursing.blogs.com/medscape_nursing/what_i_do/index.html

Gordon, S. (2005). *Nursing Against the Odds: How Health Care Cost-Cutting, Media Stereotypes, and Medical Hubris Undermine Nursing and Patient Care.* Cornell University Press.

Gosline, M.B. (2004). "Leadership in nursing education: voices from the past." *Nurs Leadershp Forum.* 2004 Winter; 9(2):51-9.

Institute of Medicine (IOM) (2004). *In the Nation's Compelling Interest: Ensuring Diversity in the Health Care Workforce.* Washington, D.C.: National Academies Press.

International Council of Nurses (2006). *Code of ethics and other information.* www.icn.ch. Geneva, Switzerland

Michael K. (2005). *What I do.* Medscape nursing blog. medscapenursing.blogs.com/medscape_nursing/what_i_do/index.html

Mims, J.A. (2005) *What I do.* Medscape nursing blog. medscapenursing.blogs.com/medscape_nursing/what_i_do/index.html

Naylor, H. (2005). *What I do.* Medscape nursing blog. medscapenursing.blogs.com/medscape_nursing/what_i_do/index.html

Poslusny, S.M. (1989). "Feminist friendship: Isabel Hampton Robb, Lavinia Lloyd Dock and Mary Adelaide Nutting." *Image, Journal of Nursing Scholarship,* 21(2):63-8.

Sohn P.M. & Loveland Cook C.A. (2002) "Nurse practitioner knowledge of complementary alternative health care: foundation for practice." *Journal of Advanced Nursing* 39(1), 9-12.

Spetz, J. (2002). "The value of education in a licensed profession: the choice of associate or baccalaureate degrees in nursing.*" Economics of Education Review,* 21(1), 73-85.

U.S. Department of Health and Human Services, Division of Nursing (2005). *Registered Nurse Population: Preliminary Findings from the Eighth National Sample Survey of Registered Nurses, March 2004.* A random survey done every four years containing salary, demographic, educational, role, and title information on 2.2 million registered nurses. bhpr.hrsa.gov/healthworkforce/reports/rnsurvey/default.htm

Werley, H. H., Devine, E. C, Zorn, C.R., Ryan, P., & Westra, B.L. (1991). "The Nursing Minimum Data Set: Abstraction tool for standardized, comparable, essential data," *American Journal of Public Health,* 81, 421-426.

Werley, H. H., & Lang, N.M. (Eds.) (1988). *Identification of the Nursing Minimum Data Set.* New York: Springer.

Visit Vault at **www.vault.com** for insider company profiles, expert advice, career message boards, expert resume reviews, the Vault Job Board and more.

VAULT CAREER LIBRARY

91

Web Resources

Useful web links from www.gem-nursing.org/Aboutnursing.php

American Assembly for Men in Nursing
www.aamn.org

American Association of Colleges of Nursing
www.aacn.nche.edu

American Association of Critcal Care Nurses
www.aacn.org

American Association of Occupational Health Nurses
www.aaohn.org

American Nurses Association
www.nursingworld.org

Asian American/ Pacific Islander Nurses Association
www.aapina.org

Association of Women's Health, Obstetric and Neonatal Nurses
www.awhonn.org

Career Voyages
www.careervoyages.gov

Choose Nursing
www.choosenursing.com

Developmental Disabilities Nurses Association
www.ddna.org

Discover Nursing
www.discovernursing.com

Entrepreneurial Networking Group for Nurses
www.engn.org

Exceptional Nurse
www.exceptionalnurse.com

Inova Nursing Mentorship Program
www.inova.org/inovapublic.srt/careers/fellowships/mentorship.htm

Massachusetts Association of Registered Nurses
www.marnonline.org

Massachusetts Center for Nursing
www.nursema.org

MetaNurse
www.metanurse.com/index2.html

Minority Nurse
www.minoritynurse.com/academic/index.html

National Alaska Native American Indian Nurses Association
www.nanaina.com

National Association of Hispanic Nurses
www.thehispanicnurses.org

National Black Nurses Association
www.nbna.org

National Coalition of Ethnic Minority Nurse Associations
www.ncemna.org

National League of Nursing
www.nln.org

Nurse Recruiter
www.nurse-recruiter.com

Nurse Zone
www.nursezone.com

Nurses for a Healthier Tomorrow
www.nursesource.org

NurseWeek
www.nurseweek.com

Nursing Schools
www.allnursingschools.com

Philippine Nurses Association of America
www.pnaa03.org

Princeton Review—Nursing Career Profiles
www.princetonreview.com/cte/profiles/dayinLife.asp?careerID=100

Sigma Theta Tau International Honor Society of Nursing
www.nursingsociety.org

Tennessee Health Careers
www.tnhealthcareers.com

Visit Vault at **www.vault.com** for insider company profiles, expert advice,
career message boards, expert resume reviews, the Vault Job Board and more.

VAULT CAREER LIBRARY

93

The Center for Nursing Advocacy
www.nursingadvocacy.org

The National Student Nurses Association
www.nsna.org

U.S. Department of Labor, Bureau of Labor Statistics
www.bls.gov/oco/ocos083.htm

U.S. Department of Labor, Bureau of Labor Statistics: Statistics on Registered Nurses
www.dol.gov/wb/factsheets/Qf-nursing.htm

About the Author

Melinda Jenkins, PhD, FNP has over 20 years' experience as a family nurse practitioner as well as more than 15 years' teaching experience. She currently teaches in the doctoral program at Seton Hall and lives in New York.

Visit Vault at **www.vault.com** for insider company profiles, expert advice, career message boards, expert resume reviews, the Vault Job Board and more.

VAULT CAREER LIBRARY 95

Use the Internet's
MOST TARGETED
job search tools.

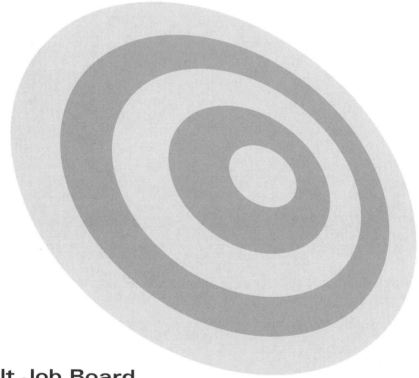

Vault Job Board

Target your search by industry, function and experience level, and find the job openings that you want.

VaultMatch Resume Database

Vault takes matchmaking to the next level: post your resume and customize your search by industry, function, experience and more. We'll match job listings with your interests and criteria and e-mail them directly to your inbox.